RoadFrames

Kris Lackey

RoadFrames

The
American
Highway
Narrative

University of Nebraska Press, Lincoln and London

© 1997 by the University of
Nebraska Press. All rights
reserved. Manufactured in the
United States of America.
⊗ The paper in this book meets
the minimum requirements of
American National Standard for
Information Science—
Permanence of Paper for Printed
Library Materials,
ANSI Z39.48-1984. Library of
Congress Cataloging-in-
Publication Data. Lackey, Kris,
1953–   RoadFrames : the
American highway narrative /
Kris Lackey.   p.   cm. Includes
bibliographic references and
index. ISBN 0-8032-2924-0
(alk. paper). 1. Travelers'
writings, American—History and
criticism. 2. American prose
literature—20th century—History
and criticism. 3. American fiction
—20th century—history and
criticism. 4. Automobile travel—
United States—Historiography.
5. Express highways—United
States—Historiography.
6. Quests (Expeditions) in
literature. 7. Americans—Travel—
Historiography. 8. Automobile
travel in literature. 9. Express
highways in literature. 10. Travel
in literature. 11. Narration
(Rhetoric). I. Title.
PS366.T 73133 1997
810.9'355—dc21
96-49443 CIP

To Karleene Smith and Susan Smith Lackey
and to a few of my many fine teachers:
Jim Barbour, Bill Mitchell, Bill McPheron,
Bob Clarke, Morris Eaves, Edith Buchanan,
Madge Randolph, Myrtle Seright, and
Gene Frumkin. They are democrats.

CONTENTS

PREFACE

This book is mostly an extended meditation on the shadow texts of American road books written between 1903 and 1994. By shadow texts I mean both the unacknowledged traditions that shape these books and the ignored or repressed antithetical messages that lie beneath the authors' assertions. In some cases road writers peer into these shadow texts — their own and those of other writers. Most thoughtful road writers of nonfiction want to understand what it means to hurtle in relative privacy across a recently settled country. Their coming to terms with both the new medium of automotive travel and the American landscape is a process of superimposing upon what they see paradigms learned from books or culture or experience. Novelists likewise want to see how this new medium affects their characters. Since the flourishing of the novel in the eighteenth century, perhaps only a half dozen new cultural forces, such as democracy and industrialism, have altered social patterns and the sense of self more than the automobile.

Many of the books I talk about are unfamiliar and scarce. They were retrieved from big libraries like the Huntington and from small-town public libraries in Missouri and Georgia. Others are the first that come to mind when the topic is broached. More road novels than nonfiction narratives have survived in public memory and in print, and this is as it should be.

By and large the nonfiction books are sluggish and cliché ridden. Some are bigoted. By intuition and surmise, I winnowed from nine decades of nonfiction road books fifty or so whose reviews or titles intimated at least a smudge of sense. Many of these are rich works of travel. Possibly I have overlooked fine books. If so, I will be happy to learn of them. Though I discuss about fifteen novels, I have focused on nonfiction books, partly because they have been so neglected and partly because Cynthia Dettelbach's *In the Driver's Seat* has already capably examined automotive themes in familiar highbrow writers.

This study is neither exhaustive nor completely systematic. Rather it is thematic and ruminant. I have tried to address a general audience. The amateur, who by definition reads road books for the love of reading them, may enjoy learning about the various literary traditions that have shaped them. The literary scholar, who already knows about the picaresque and the pastoral, naturalism and Transcendentalism, can bypass the hornbook to these traditions early in the introduction and move directly to discussions of the narratives themselves.

By and large I have not engaged longstanding debates about western history, automotive history, and literary classics like *On the Road* and *The Grapes of Wrath*, though I have drawn from scholars in several disciplines. My purpose has been instead to retrieve some forgotten books, set them alongside more familiar ones, and open new territory for critical discussion.

In the bargain, I argue that the twentieth-century car traveler views his or her journey as a symbolic gesture in which the individual confronts and interprets larger forces that have shaped a moment in the life of the nation. With some weighty exceptions, this tension generally amplifies the personal while it consolidates and simplifies cultural information. A moving automobile naturally supplies, beyond its windshield, more surface than depth. The tradition of Romantic travel, emphasizing as it does the impressions, emotions, reflections, and imagination of the traveler, is auspicious to this glut of surface. And so it often happens that the search for personal context is not so much a search as an expression of sensibility playing out over the land, unchecked by the knotted pasts of discrete places.

The symbolic gesture, though—that is the thing. Perhaps it is the space that does it, or the speed, enhancing the eye's power to consume and the individual's perceived power to master terrain. In any case, the traveler often believes that driving somehow bestows disinterested liberty, a temporary and privileged innocence of the forces that have made automobiles and highways, even blue ones, possible. African American travelers also see their journeys as symbolic undertakings but cannot enjoy an illusion of disinterested liberty. Their travels, beset by fear and harassment, balk fantasies of a spatial escape from historical forces.

In the seven novels I treat in the last chapter, car voyaging remains a symbolic gesture, describing in spatial terms a character's education in or flight from domesticity. The household, whether depicted as haven or hell, in turn represents larger ideals. The road can temper the protagonist for marriage, in which case it serves a domestic ideal. It can also threaten or destroy marriage, in which case it subverts the domestic ideal and all it represents—monogamy, self-sacrifice, workplace slavery, and stasis.

The great American road has become a magic screen for the fears and desires of travelers with means and light skin—most who have written about it. Automobiles have defeated the road's instructive friction, rendered it cinematic and pliable to mythmaking. The road absorbs and reflects much more readily than it stumps, which is why we concoct such ponderous excuses to travel it.

ACKNOWLEDGMENTS

I would like to thank Maria McGarrity and Angela Beerman, Research Assistants at the University of New Orleans, for their patience and discrimination as they helped me pore through a century of reviews and book lists in search of promising road books. The library faculty at UNO, whose omniscience God will not begrudge, opened shortcuts and located rare books from everywhere with alacrity and unfailing goodwill. In particular I owe big debts to Connie Phelps and Jeannine Gelpi in Interlibrary Loan and to Johnny Powers, Steve Alleman, and Bob Heriard in Reference. A number of my colleagues brought road books to my attention: John Cooke, Young Smith, John Hazlett, Carl Malmgren, Stuart Stelly, Michael Higgins, Kim McDonald, Steve Choisser, Carol Antosiak, Howard Darlington, Anne Smith, Joel Morgan, Charlie Bishop, Doug Brinkley, and others I may have forgotten. John Cooke and Doug Brinkley read and critiqued sections of the manuscript. Peggy Baker greased the wheels of the academy, and Kathleen Bowman provided clerical support. Mr. Gary Kurutz at the Sacramento branch of the California State Library and Mrs. Amelia Bliss helped me locate the first transcontinental highway narrative, *From Ocean to Ocean in a Winton*; the staff of the Huntington Library provided me a photocopy of it. The staffs of several libraries at Tulane University courteously helped me locate several obscure works. The University of New Orleans granted me a sabbatical to work on this project.

My UNO students in English 6007, The American Highway Narrative, challenged my ideas, and they supplied several original ones in the bargain. For their engagement, energy, originality, and inspiration, I humbly thank them.

RoadFrames

INTRODUCTION

The first published account of a transcontinental automobile journey appeared only thirty-three years after the death of the last surviving member of the Lewis and Clark expedition. And Sergeant Patrick Gass was by no means the youngest soldier in the Corps of Discovery.

In the summer of 1903 Horatio Nelson Jackson and his chauffeur, Sewall Crocker, piloted a Winton two-seater from San Francisco to New York, a trip that took sixty-three days (Patton 42). Jackson recounted this first auto trek across the United States in *From Ocean to Ocean in a Winton*. He and Crocker passed a few hundred miles south of the Little Bighorn, where Custer had died only twenty-seven summers before, then south of the Sioux reservation where Sitting Bull was killed just over a dozen years earlier—in 1890, the year the Census Department declared the frontier closed (Duncan 375). In 1923, twenty years after Jackson's crossing, the first transcontinental national highway (a route traversable since the teens) was finished: Route 30, the Lincoln Highway, which crossed former Shoshoni, Wind River, Omaha, Pawnee, Oto, Missouri, and Iowa ranges (Patton 44, Webb 51). It struck the Missouri River almost precisely where Meriwether Lewis first addressed a gathering of Plains Indians from the Oto and Missouri tribes.

Less than a dozen years after Route 30 opened for business, some writers taking the wheel for cross-country trips began to eulogize the frontier and measure the cost of its conquest, even as their border crossings were sped by a vast concert of technology and manufacture. Indeed, in little more than a long lifetime after Jefferson had dispatched Lewis and Clark to find the mythic Northwest Passage, most of the tribes the Corps encountered had been decimated by war and disease, the buffalo had almost been exterminated, much of the Great Plains was "settled," fenced, and crosshatched with railroads—and flivvers were jolting over the Great Divide.

Routes followed by the pioneering "machines," as early automobiles were called, often lay over bison traces and trails etched by Native American travois. They paralleled the rails that had recently preceded them, revived stage roads abandoned for the railroad, and hugged rivers not long before plied by sternwheelers, many of which were themselves displaced by trains. But even the earliest highways sometimes left nature's paths of least resistance to follow the abstract lines of the surveyor—those township gridlines, first imposed by the Land Ordinance of 1785, which, reified as section roads, became the intaglio signature of private property across the Midwest and the Great Plains (Jackson, *American Space*, 61). The automobile, its Western trails smoothed first by capitalist boosters, then by government, recapitulated Anglo American exploration and conquest of the far West astonishingly soon after the fact. It arrived too late there to be of any military use, but only just. In 1915 *Scribner's* printed side-by-side articles about motorized combat in France and automobile gypsying in the Sierras, and trucks were used in the American campaign against Pancho Villa. A concrete grease rack still stands forlornly in the desert south of Columbus, New Mexico, a town raided by Villa in 1916.[1] The automobile arrived in the West after military exploits and atrocities had already been mythicized and commercialized by dime novels and Wild West shows. Versions of the latter were still available to early motorists in the form of rodeos and Harvey House entertainments. Emily Post, en route to San Francisco around 1915, was entertained by Indian

1. See articles in the February 1915 *Scribner's* by Freeston and Belden.

dances at the Alvarado Hotel in Albuquerque (167), and as late as 1933 a Crazy Horse imposter fooled roving columnist Lewis Gannett at a Sheridan rodeo (183).

Unlike the repeating rifle or even the locomotive, the automobile was, as far as the American West was concerned, an innocent machine when it arrived. It did not help win the West; and so in its early days, when western Native Americans had just begun to be romanticized and pitied, it was not tainted by combat. Although the West was already "pacified," outside the railroad hotels it was packaged only in myth. Its forbidding terrain remained intact and its human types—cowboys, Indians, sodbusters— still there for the motoring vagabond to view from a jolting tonneau. "Still trudge the prairie schooners," Sinclair Lewis wrote in his motoring novel *Free Air* (1919); "cowpunchers still stand at the doors of log cabins" (121). Following Coronado's sixteenth-century route through Arizona, Winifred Dixon recounted, in 1921, the motives of others (including Indians) who had passed that way: "blood-lust and gold-lust, religion, fanaticism, and empire building" (90). Like many motoring writers, she claimed to be an innocent sojourner, free-floating, disinterested, and untarnished by history. The West, she said, was "still new to the motoring tourist" (4), who could bask in "the romance of a thousand years" (90).

The pioneer motorists passed through long-settled regions on the way to the West, but no other part of the country, with the possible exception of the Deep South, has laid so wide a claim to the transcontinental driver's imagination. Here the new and celebrated freedom of individual mechanical travel almost caught up with the frontier. Early motorists drew close to the forces that for good or ill had forged their land, and if they considered it at all they felt they were traveling outside the giant corporate rail and commodity network that exploited the West's natural resources (Trachtenberg 19–37). Like the trappers and clerics and soldiers who had come before, they traveled with crude maps or none at all and braved cruel terrain and crueller weather. Yet from the start they were spectators, insulated and relatively safe, symbolically reenacting the discovery and conquest of their nation. Railroad passengers, as many motoring travelers pointed out, were denied this experience. Not only were they bound by unwanted society, speed, and fixed routes, they were just too comfortable. They could not taste the weather or appreciate the mud and rain-swollen rivers braved by the first settlers. And they could not be left to their own thoughts. With some modification, this railroad/highway contrast is reborn in the Interstate/blue highways split of more recent highway books.

The rhetoric of discovery—issuing from the wish to reenact pioneer hardships, to recreate an innocent country, and to imaginatively possess the land—remains vital after almost a century of American nonfiction automotive narratives and road novels. This impulse is strongest in the West, which approximates the early "emptiness" of the rest of the country and offers the illusion of discovery; but it translates easily into projections in more settled regions of a bygone era that can be visited in the imagination. The old myths, it seems, are still busy. But the automobile, whose pilots are so often soaked in these myths, is a machine that requires a complicated, extensive, and costly support network involving design, production, distribution, repair, fuel, and highways. Such a network could be said merely to reproduce that of the railroad, or the paddlewheeler, or even, more abstractly, the process of moving goods and people en masse farther west.

But shortly after the very early years of motoring, when drivers called their cars "machines" and spent hours of every day repairing them, the automobile began to slough its mechanical identity. Perhaps because it offered autonomy from the railroad and took people out of manufacturing centers, it seemed to provide quick access to the countryside and escape from the strictures associated with both industry and mass transportation. The automobile was a machine so perfectly responsive to individual whim that it assumed the neutrality of a prosthesis, like binoculars or the tinted Claude glasses once donned by sightseers who wished to transform landscapes into Claude Lorrain paintings. And because it is sometimes metaphorically linked to the body, it could function as a machine while its mechanical attributes were naturalized, made to seem part of nature. It became a kind of green machine, unlike the steam shovel, smelter furnace, combine, or cattle car that exploited Western resources. The reenactment of exploration and the willed illusion of discovery and conquest were not smudged by manufacture. They were not the labor-saving issue of mass production but the "genuine" accomplishment of motoring pioneers, even when those pioneers were driving across the United States in the 1980s.

Among the many road-book topics and conventions issuing from this early yearning to reenact discovery and possession, it is a short step to Transcendental motoring—"Thoreau at 29 cents a gallon" (Belasco 107) as one early auto gypsy proclaimed. If the automobile freed one physically from the confines of the city and the railroad and allowed one to write "whim" on the runningboard, intellectually it was peculiarly auspicious to the surviving tenets of New England Transcendentalism. This heady brand of American idealistic philosophy taught independence of mind, scepticism toward convention, the value of rural retreat in the recovery of neglected mental forms, the reciprocity of mind and matter, the richness of folkways and folk speech, and the unfettered play of imagination upon the natural world. In even the least literary of American road books, the departing vagabonds might be sent on their way with a Whitman salute. More philosophical writers, like Robert Pirsig (who takes along a copy of *Walden*) and William Least Heat-Moon (who takes Whitman's *Leaves of Grass*), fleshed out the Transcendental implications of motoring, discoursing at length on the benefits of shunning routine, observing nature close up, following impulse and the less-traveled road, living frugally and simply, exulting in the variety of American landscape and pursuits, and provisionally rejecting bourgeois respectability. That such desiderata should be linked with the automobile shows how the rhetoric of motor travel transforms the machine at its center into a prosthesis of consciousness—artificial but so well fitted to the human mind and body that it all but disappears.

The Transcendental possibilities of motoring lie beneath most philo-sophical driving, not only the rolling examinations of self (as it relates to family, society, politics, aesthetics, and history) so common in the road book, but also the mock- or anti-Transcendental ruminations of drivers who either spoof the conventions of highway writing or expose its ideological biases. In the last camp are writers who reveal the economic and racial prerequisites for proper Transcendental motoring. Notable among these writers are black travelers like John A. Williams and Chet Fuller who cannot entertain a Whitmanesque enthusiasm for the open road, yet who are, like Ralph Waldo Ellison, consumed by that old Transcendentalist problem, the location and nature of the essential self and its relationship to social power structures. Books of a decidedly anthropological or historical cast may limit or altogether omit self-consciousness as a topic, in which case they lie off the Transcendental road. They are object-driven rather than subject-driven. Also outside this context are the white-glove narratives concerned primarily with the nature and quality of accommodations. Because almost every road writer is occupied at one time or another with such practical matters, travelers who don't fare much beyond them illuminate all consumer subtexts, including the connection between discovering America and consuming America.

The "Transcendental" rubric is useful for marking a large category of highway writings that share certain qualities and postures traceable to the larger Romantic movement in literature, of which Transcendentalism was an issue. Though their works are not so immediately influential as those of Whitman, Emerson, and Thoreau, the autobiographies of Rousseau, Goethe, and Wordsworth (in *The Prelude*), the Gothic road passages from the fiction of De La Motte Fouque, William Godwin, and other writers in the genre, and Romantic travel works such as Washington Irving's *A Tour on the Prairies* have all left their marks on American road books by affirming the power of individual subjectivity and imagination to create many worlds out of one. This legacy of Romanticism in general and American Transcendentalism in particular—a preoccupation with individual consciousness as a shaping force that is in turn shaped by experience—ultimately yields not only the general autobiographical elements of American road books, in which highway episodes may alter awareness, recall events in the driver's life, or symbolically recreate wishes or fears, but also the more particular discussions of "highway consciousness," states of mind peculiar to driving that range from blankness to fantasy to temporary psychosis.

In the same vein is writing we might call road phenomenology, discussions of how things outside the windshield are perceived by the speeding eye. This theme is broached by such writers as William Saroyan, Kaj Klitgaard, and Jean Baudrillard.

There are countless other forms and traditions, ranging from the ancient *Epic of Gilgamesh* to serial television dramas like *Route 66*, underwriting the modern road book. Eric Leed's trenchant study of the enduring themes and structures of travel writing, *The Mind of the Traveler* (1991), situates the beginning of modern travel well before the Romantic period in the chivalric journey, which was "essentially self-referential, undertaken to reveal the essential character of the knight as 'free'" (12). Unlike the heroic wanderer of earlier epics, compelled by the gods to endure the hardships of travel, the knight chose his journey as an "opportunity to demonstrate an identity—as freedom, self-display, and self-discovery" (13). This gesture, which anticipated both the voyages of discovery and the advent of tourism, contained the germ of Romantic travel, with its emphasis on "indeterminacy," "autonomy," and, once again, self-discovery (13).

Humbler than the knight-errant and arising in the period of his decline, the roguish picaro or picara is another literary ancestor of some modern travel personae. A descendent of the ancient trickster figure, the picaro emerged as a complete literary type in sixteenth-century Spanish fiction, notably in the anonymous *Lazarillo de Tormes* and Mateo Alemán's *Guzmán de Alfarache*, and was adopted by French, German, English and, much later, American writers. Huckleberry Finn is the most famous American example. A low-born man without means, the picaro is a wanderer who must live by menial work and cunning. He is often alienated both materially and spiritually from governing classes, and he may wield a sardonic wit. Lazarillo, Ann Kaler observes, "represents the death of the feudal system and the inhospitability of the industrial systems to non-productive workers" (15). The picara descends to us from the fictional sixteenth-century Spanish bawds Lozana, created by Francisco Delicado, and Celestina, created by Fernando de Rojas, by way of Cervantes's Dulcinea and Defoe's Moll Flanders (Kaler 23–24). Sharing most of the picaro's qualities, she may additionally use her sexual charms to get along in the world.

As the picaresque novel developed as a form, it came to be marked by a loose, episodic structure built around the adventures of the protagonist, frank treatment of vulgar speech and events, and scant character development. Though in recent years this definition has lost some of its precision as "picaresque" has been applied to any narrative of rolling adventure, its more exact terms can apply to either fictional or nonfictional American road books in which the protagonist is cast as a resourceful and sometimes even hapless vagabond living on the edge. In fiction, Dos Passos's Fainy McCreary in *The 42nd Parallel* (1930), Nelson Algren's Dove Linkhorn in *A Walk on the Wild Side* (1956), Kerouac's Sal Paradise and Dean Moriarty in *On the Road* (1957), B. Traven's Gales in *The Cotton-Pickers* (1969?), Katherine Dunn's Jean Gillis in *Truck* (1971), and Jim Dodge's George Gastin in *Not Fade Away* (1987) exemplify the surviving type—outsiders whose hardscrabble road-lives fit them for roles as satirists and enemies of settled bourgeois life. Some road writers who enjoy the security of middle-class travel adopt the picaro posture to create the illusion that their experiences, and not merely their ideas, have set them against mainstream American ideology. Others allude to picaresque literature out of pure drollery, as does Steinbeck when he calls his camper "Rocinante" after Quixote's horse.

Of the three remaining literary traditions that come into play in this book—the pastoral, American literary naturalism, and the early travel book about the United States—the pastoral figures most prominently. Dating back to Theocritus's sketches of rustic life in the *Idylls* about 300 B.C. and the eclogues of Virgil, in which shepherds engage in singing matches, the pastoral as a conventionalized mode descends to us by way of centuries of English poetry beginning with the classical revival of the Renaissance and continuing with many permutations through the Romantic period and into our own age.

The pastoral poem, story, or interlude is set in a peaceful rural place, away from the confusion and noise of the city. There simple, contented, innocent country folk talk of love and toodle on their flutes, or jaded city dwellers come to escape urban distractions and, by immersing themselves in rural beauty, restore their spirits with meditation. The rise of urban industry could be credited with reawakening and redefining the pastoral myth when the conventions of pastoral poetry had grown hackneyed and ridiculous, for the city teeming with dark satanic mills and gaunt millhands threw the agricultural landscape and its "contented" inhabitants into starker relief. Though not all English Romantic and pre-Romantic poets idealized the lives of rural laborers, some Romantic poets, Wordsworth chief among them, rejuvenated pastoral impulses and oppositions by restating the city/country split and by complicating the act of perceiving nature. The great lyrical nature poems of the early nineteenth century strip away the pasteboard conventions of the pastoral and create a wider range of personal responses to nature in complexes of memory, emotion, desire, loss, and philosophical idealism. But while Romanticism bequeathed to us a more sophisticated rhetoric of response to nature than that offered by the older pastoral, it perpetuated that myth's most powerful element: the opposed spiritual conditions of urban and rural places.

When the pastoral myth is mistaken for reality or exerts undue influence on an interpretation of an economy or a society, it becomes part of ideology—another of the "natural," unacknowledged models we use to judge what we see. As Raymond Williams has demonstrated, this process, by which farm work is viewed as something undertaken by simple and contented folk, has had serious material consequences. It has, for example, masked the organized exploitation of British agricultural labor and contributed to Stalin's cruel suppression of the rural peasantry. In America the familiar early articulations of the pastoral ideal by Jefferson and the French Tory Crevecoeur located the yeoman farmer at the moral center of America by virtue of his economic independence and his intimate bond with nature. He thinks clearly and acts morally because he is taught by nature and not by the court or city.

More than half a century later, general public support for rapid industrial and rail development, as Leo Marx has shown, shunted critics like John Orvis, who warned that the equality of "beautiful pastoral life" would be sacrificed for a new caste system and "oppressive factory life" (qtd. in Marx 216). The Transcendentalists, whose ethics and epistemology were rooted in pastoral Romanticism, nonetheless responded to the rise of industry in unpredictable ways. Thoreau devoted most of *Walden* (1854) to examination of the intellectual and spiritual decay caused by redundant work and blind dependence on technology, including the railroad; yet even as he urged his readers to sharpen their thinking and language with an immersion in nature, he celebrated the audacity and ingenuity of rail-borne commerce (110–11). Emerson, as Marx has made plain, thought that American industrialism would not re-create here, as critics like Orvis feared, the foul Dickensian cities of Europe, but rather would grow organically from the American garden and be tempered by American space. Likewise, the railroad would open up the American landscape, especially the West, enlivening and expanding the Transcendental imagination (Marx 234–39; Emerson, "The Young American"). Whitman, an occasional Transcendentalist whose vision was more urban than that of the Concord group, gave poetic voice to Emerson's hope that mechanical locomotion would unify far-flung parts of America and the world. "Passage to India" from *Leaves of Grass* exalts the accomplishments of engineers, architects, and machinists who cause "the lands to be welded together" (2:35):

> I see over my own continent the Pacific railroad surmounting every
> barrier,
> I see the continual train of cars winding along the Platte . . .
> I cross the Laramie plains, I note the rocks in grotesque shapes, the
> buttes,

I see the plentiful larkspur and wild onions, the barren, colorless
sage-deserts . . .
(3:14–17)

The scope of Whitman's western catalogue expands dramatically into
images of world unity made possible by ships and trains.

Emerson and Whitman, then, by creating a place for the locomotive
in pastoral contemplation of the American landscape and by qualifying
the conventional opposition of machine and rural nature, prepared the
way for motorists who, like Theodore Dreiser, would contend that the
automobile even more effectively than the train brought Americans into
"intimate contact with woodland silences" and "grassy slopes" (93). Although Emerson's optimistic predictions about the future of machines
in America may have found illusory fulfillment in the automobile, manufacturing did in the end build grimy, crowded cities here. Today the
pastoral opposition of city and country thrives, as does the myth that rural
people, while no longer simpletons, indeed live simpler, healthier, more
authentic, and more contemplative lives than their urban counterparts.

Twentieth-century American road literature owes some of its darker
passages to the tradition of literary naturalism, which dramatizes biological and environmental determinism. The influence of naturalism in
this country surged just before the advent of the motor narrative and
persisted in later proletarian road sagas such as Steinbeck's *The Grapes of
Wrath* (1939), Jim Thompson's *Rough Neck* (1954), and Dos Passos's *The
42nd Parallel*. In early naturalistic works, Stephen Crane, Dreiser, Kate
Chopin, Jack London, Upton Sinclair, and Frank Norris brought the biological theories of Darwin and Thomas Huxley to bear upon plots and
characters in their novels. The typical result is a story like Crane's *Maggie: A Girl of the Streets* (1893), in which the accidents of a character's birth
and circumstances render her will and desires pointless. When applied to
later works, "naturalism" may be bound up with Marxist theories of economic oppression, the psychological determinism of Freud, or any force
in nature that supersedes will.

Somehow the automobile coursing through books with names like

On the Road, *Free Air*, and *Sweet Land* seems out of place in the naturalistic design. In most road literature the car is an existentialist's machine, built for surmounting our biological limitations, heeding our wills, escaping the gravity of work and caste—for challenging both nature and nurture. Yet the recreational road trip story, for all its vaunted feedom and spontaneity, conceals America's parallel road universe in which African American motorists have been compelled to drive at night, consult the black-focused magazine *Travelguide* for motels that accept them, and eat standing up at "nigger-windows" (Williams, *My Country* 67), a universe in which the very poor of any race travel as refugees living at the mercy of their machines and the police. In this context the recreational road trip doesn't so much create freedom as express freedom that already exists by virtue of class and race. Few as they are, motoring narratives that remind us of this fact draw upon the broad tenets of literary naturalism.

Eighteenth- and nineteenth-century American travelogues offer a precedent for object-driven anthropological nonfiction road books like Simone de Beauvoir's *America Day by Day* (1948) and Roland Wild's *Double-Crossing America* (1938). While such books may glance at the autobiographical significance of motor travel, the emphasis remains on cultural criticism and comparison.

Though not a travelogue itself, Tocqueville's *Democracy in America* (1835, 1840), which grew out of the author's extensive travels here in 1831–32, endures as the towering classic of its type. The French observer's theories about the effects of democracy on character have become such staples of modern social criticism that they are often mentioned without attribution. Tocqueville's journeys have recently been retraced by Richard Reeves (*American Journey: Traveling with Tocqueville in Search of "Democracy in America,"* 1982) and Eugene McCarthy (*America Revisited: 150 Years after Tocqueville*, 1978), though both authors follow the Frenchman's example and elide matters of the road.

I have already mentioned Crevecoeur, another French author of travel books about America, the most famous of which is *Letters from an Amer-*

ican Farmer (1782). Like Tocqueville after him, Crevecoeur traveled the land to discover how region and politics formed the character of Americans. Accordingly, Crevecoeur found the Allegheny vanguard lawless, the yeoman farmers of the northern rural settlements industrious and tolerant, the Nantucket mariners bold and enterprising, the southern slaveholders languid and dissolute. In the tradition of the most fetching travel writers, he married booming generalities with poignant anecdotes of ordinary life, a strategy that may account for his continued popularity. Two recent British visitors, James Morris in the fifties (*As I Saw the U.S.A.*, 1956) and Jonathan Raban in the nineties (*Hunting Mister Heartbreak*, 1991), take Crevecoeur ("heartbreak") along as a companion.

Among the most literate successors of Tocqueville and Crevecoeur as travelers in America are Frances Trollope, Charles Dickens, Francis Parkman, and Washington Irving, who brought to the landscape and society they found in the new republic a spectrum of influential models and sensibilities. The redoubtable Frances Trollope, a British Tory who singed the American character in her *Domestic Manners of the Americans* (1839), was not the first wayfarer in America with a gift for satire, but she was certainly the most imposing. Her twentieth-century counterparts, among them Henry Miller (*The Air-Conditioned Nightmare*, 1945), Vladimir Nabokov (through the refugee pedophile Humbert Humbert in *Lolita*, 1955), Mary Day Winn (*Macadam Trail*, 1931), and Bill Bryson (*The Lost Continent*, 1989), express their discontent in darker, more Juvenalian terms. In *American Notes* (1842), a record of his first tour in that same year, Dickens vented his disappointment at the shortcomings of American democracy, which in his view had spawned a society beset by greed and characterized by a dull uniformity of character, outspoken ignorance, and political rancor. His legacies to later travelers in the United States are a hectic impressionism, which transmogrified landscape and people into symbols of his cultural judgment, and a prevailing melancholy, which could give way to yearning for the pastoral innocence and harmony enjoyed by American Indians before the onslaught of a rapacious culture. This historical nostalgia resurfaces in modern books like Zephine Humphrey's *Green Mountains to Sierras* (1936) and William Least Heat-Moon's *Blue Highways* (1982).

Both Irving and Parkman rode horseback to the West, and their books, *A Tour on the Prairies* and *The Oregon Trail* (1849), implicitly advance this rigorous course because it toughens one's body and spirit and helps the witness of westward expansion identify with its participants. In fact, this proto–Teddy Roosevelt posture belied Parkman's frequent bouts with nervous diarrhea and his disgust for the pioneers he met, and it hid Irving's petulance, inept campcraft, and snobbery. The discrepancy between posture and personality does not generally survive in twentieth-century nonfiction road books as a broad discrepancy between the robust western pilgrim and the urbane critic. Modern writers admit their weaknesses more readily. What nineteenth-century western adventurer would have confessed, as Peter S. Beagle did in 1965, that he was "a shy and chicken person" (154)? In subtler variations, though, the habit persists. People on the road often view themselves as changed by virtue of their perceived independence from work and home. Whereas Irving and Parkman sought to join the national enterprise, their modern counterparts often reject it. But in either case the journey carries a symbolic weight as the persona, the mask created by the author, is fashioned in accord with the trip's symbolism.

This sketch of the road-book's traditions shows first of all that no road book is cut from the whole cloth of any tradition. Most, like Clancy Sigal's autobiographical road novel *Going Away* (1961), draw from traditions as old as the picaresque and as new as the Beats. Sigal's novel tells the story of a symbolic journey in which the narrator, as he crosses the country in good picaresque trim, grapples with his alienation from the friends he visits and from his nation, which has ignored "even the wannest of Thoreau's strictures and dreams" (361). He had first taken the road west when he was young, drawn by the romantic promise of discovering the frontier "as it had once looked to Marquette and Pike and Fremont and Big Bill Haywood" (97). As a roving labor organizer he knew his place in the world and had a personality to go with it—tough, sensitive, uncompromising. Now moving eastward through and finally away from America in the fifties, he finds the West sullied by development and his friends politically apathetic and resigned to middle-class life. Finished as a labor organizer, hopeless about the political Left, spiritually awash, he drives, as he says, "on the landscape of my temper," a refugee driven not by economic need like the Okies but by "cultural" necessity (365). The road does free him to mull his historical identity, but his meditations only lead him to conclude that he cannot sustain the road's fluidity, its gift of independence from a culture he despises. His road quest for a new sense of self is a failure, yet as a gesture, as a symbol of his loss, it generalizes personal misery into cultural indictment. When the narrator was younger, the road had crystallized his personality because the far West, its landscape and Anglo history, answered his sense of self, trait for trait: he was a groundbreaker, a resolute "working-class hero" (504). The same road, because it is largely a mental product, now reflects his disintegration and despair.

Before taking leave of America, however, the narrator gets one more shot at road joy, a chance to recover, if only briefly, the promise of his earlier western journey. This Romantic pastoral interlude, though it reverses the usual compass points, has a familiar ring. The driver enters fresh territory, in this case Massachusetts: "I felt *now, now my life is changing*. Nobody knows me here. I can be anything I want. . . . I felt *young*, rolling up over the yellow leaf-matted hills, the countryside in the morning one riotous, blending explosion after another of Constable colors . . . the slim untraveled road an inch thick with fallen yellow and light brown leaves . . . very reassuring after that night on the Turnpike" (392). For all its epiphanic ardor, this is the most conventional expression in American road literature—the pastoral transition from turnpike to lane, the shedding of old connections, the prospect of a new identity, the reclamation of youth. In Sigal's book, however, this unmistakably American confidence in new places is voiced by a narrator who has lost faith in everything else. Having traveled thousands of miles with him and learned the measure of his discontent, we can see the graveyard he's whistling past and understand the social and political sources of his malaise. Without the richness of context Sigal affords, road epiphanies often conceal the boredom or anger that fosters them. They seem unearned, transitory, and inconsequential.

The cheap epiphany leads to a thicket of contradictions in American road writing. The traveler obeys the Transcendental call to step outside routine, rediscover the roots of intellect in nature, and expand the imagination with images from the American wilderness. Yet one Transcendental chore modern road writers generally shun is denaturalizing both the automobile and the infrastructure creating and sustaining it. They would rather exempt it from their cultural criticism because it allows them to hover outside and above, to approach and escape what they observe—Thoreau's cabin on wheels at twenty-nine cents a gallon. Like the Concord naturalist meticulously describing his cabin and cataloguing his expenses, motorists lovingly do the same for their cars, usually with the same pride in thrift and efficiency.

The automobile is a machine apart, good for autonomy and solitude, meditation and country escapes. It has also proven to be an antisocial machine that fragments families and cities and further destabilizes a nomadic citizenry. By tremendously exaggerating our mobility and power of sight, so that as we turn our wheel and gaze we scan vast surfaces, it has inflated our sense of individual power, will, and significance. It raises the threshold of novelty for its occupants as it encourages impatience and intolerance. Has it lived up to its promise as a way to get people nearer the land and its people than the train or steamboat? Yes, but only materially.

Nonfiction highway books often cultivate the illusion of intimacy, variously couched as "listening to America," "traveling the backroads," or "feeling the pulse of America," while denying the countervailing influences of regional stereotyping, historical nostalgia, superficial impressionism, and the simple quest for novelty. If the peregrine writer does not question the artificial nature of road perception, including the influence of convention and prejudice, what's usually left is an ersatz

Transcendentalism: a vague wish to "change myself or rather to find out something I didn't yet know about myself" (O'Gara 115), a paean to freedom, a pastoral epiphany. If the residual impulse lacks the intellectual rigor of the early Transcendentalists, if it seems a little too mannered at times, our road narratives would drone and sag without the promise of afflatus, a moment when the driver feels, along with Dallas Lore Sharp, "that the wheels of my being synchronized perfectly with the wheels of my going, all that was within me meshing with all that was without . . . without grabbing of the clutch" (110–11). Not quite so organic as Emerson's transparent eyeball, but respectable for a flivver in Kansas.

As the twentieth century draws to a close, a growing body of American highway literature has produced its own influential figures, notably Kerouac, Steinbeck, Heat-Moon, Robert M. Pirsig, author of *Zen and the Art of Motorcycle Maintenance* (1974), and John Howard Griffin, author of *Black Like Me* (1960–61).[2] The continued popularity of these travelers insures that no highway book written into the next century will enjoy a life entirely its own. Not only will reviewers continue to judge new road books by their predecessors, but new writers will find that the authors in their rearview mirrors are larger than they appear.[3]

But never more *numerous* than they appear. So much respectable nonfiction travel writing of this century has proven ephemeral that these few names are all that survive from a much larger roll of fellow travelers. Earlier writers establish types of road narrative that may be later taken up by writers who have not read their work: the form is circulating, but there may be no direct influence. One example is a nonfiction highway book I call the passage narrative, in which the driver-author is trying to move

2. For example, Kerouac is mentioned in Sigal (136), Wolfe (13), Raban (240), Brinkley (508), and Eighner (233); Steinbeck is mentioned in Duncan (106), Brinkley (508), and Beauvoir (*Grapes* 165); Heat-Moon is mentioned in Duncan (106) and Brinkley (508); Pirsig is mentioned in Raban (240); Griffin is mentioned in Fuller (13) and Harris (31).

3. Among a good many examples, Steinbeck is mentioned in a review of Caldwell (Pickrel), Kerouac and Steinbeck in reviews of Heat-Moon (Perrin, Fuller), and Heat-Moon in a review of Bryson (Slung).

from one stage of life to another. The road events in this narrative show the author adjusting values, opinions, and feelings in order to cope with the future. At its most dramatic, this change can take the form of an emotional and intellectual crisis. Along the road we usually discover the causes of this crisis as well as the possible ways in which it can be resolved (beyond simply taking a road trip). Recent examples of the passage narrative include Sigal's autobiographical novel, Pirsig's *Zen*, Chet Fuller's *I Hear Them Calling My Name* (1981), and sections of Heat-Moon's *Blue Highways*. In large part all these follow Richard Phenix's *On My Way Home* (1947) and Michael Robertson's *Beyond the Sunset* (1950), two soundly crafted nonfiction tales of postwar readjustment along western backroads. Yet I have never seen either Phenix or Robertson mentioned by a reviewer of one of the later books. Likewise, Chet Fuller acknowledges his debt as a black writer traveling in the South to John Howard Griffin, the white author of *Black Like Me* (13), but does not mention two other travel books by black authors, Carl Rowan's *South of Freedom* (1952) and John A. Williams's *This Is My Country Too* (1965). Like Phenix and Robertson, Rowan and Williams had already fallen out of currency.

When road writers acknowledge the influence of their modern predecessors, they view their own work either as a continuation in the same vein of others' writing or as a clear departure from it. By voicing his admiration for John Howard Griffin, Chet Fuller laid claim to the black incognito tradition in his car travels two decades later. In *Out West* Dayton Duncan proudly cribbed any number of road habits and observations from Heat-Moon and Steinbeck, crediting them by name in the bargain (106). Following Heat-Moon, for instance, he developed an elaborate slate of "road rules." That Duncan employed such conventions so freely without fear of being labeled derivative shows how quickly the form and conventions of the camper excursion outgrew their originators and formed an independent tradition.

By the late eighties the familiar postures and conventions of the camper trek were ripe for satire and inversion. The penchant for backroads (actually much older than the camper trek), the quest for authentic regional food, the commotion over outfitting, the disparagement of mass culture and the nostalgia for folkways, the lyrical nature writing—all were perfect straight-man material for a curmudgeonly traveler like Bill Bryson. The first half of *The Lost Continent* gives the raspberry to most of these road-book traits. His road rule for small-town dining, for example, is never to eat in a cafe with blood on the walls. As for the nuances of prairie landscape, "Missouri looked precisely the same as Illinois, which had looked precisely the same as Iowa" (33). And those sweet rural hamlets? In Michigan, at least, "towns were rare and mostly squalid" (183). It is a testament to the charm of the old camper trek that even Bryson falls back onto its foldout bed of conventions when his laugh machine runs out of juice. This capitulation aside, Bryson's caustic version of the backroads odyssey grows more out of his atypical road persona (a "flinty-hearted jerkoff") than out of a complete rejection of the strategy.

By contrast, Mark Winegardner's profession of road principles in *Elvis Presley Boulevard* (1987) characterizes the blue highways genre as "pompous and sentimental" (11), its writers often "backroad reactionaries and other people with time on their hands, tenure and grant money in their pockets" (117). By taking the road most traveled, the Interstate, revelling in the mass-produced food and icons along its margins, and choosing popular destinations like Graceland and Disneyland, Winegardner fashions a populist road agenda out of pure reverse snobbery. Though he has good reason to suspect the rhetorical postures of his predecessors, his own amounts to nothing without theirs. He rejects worn road-writing conventions but cannot muster new ones convincing enough to disguise his own snobbery in this retro-chic quest.

Clancy Sigal, through the narrator of *Going Away*, faults the occasional romanticism of road writers in the vein of Kerouac who mistake the "rhythm and texture and substance of the road" for "what makes up life" (136). He has concluded, after much hitchhiking experience, that life on the road for someone without means is in fact brutal. "And believe it or not, it's not that much better when you go driving. . . . because all the time you are tire-whining past fellow citizens who live walled up in their own old fears" (137). Sigal chooses Kerouac's form (the picaresque transcontinental jag) to deliver a Kerouac message (domestic bourgeois life is cowardly and stultifying), but he does not see one as an antidote for the other. If anything, *Going Away* alters the customary trajectory of most earlier road books, not only literally, as the narrator moves from west to east and out of the country, but spiritually: wandering in America is a sad and empty affair if the wayfarer doesn't believe that the self has meaning and worth only in the lovely vacuum of American space, which purifies and absolves because it banishes everything but the imagination.

Sigal's narrator does not entirely relinquish this source of joy, as we have seen, but looks beyond it to the historical situation of the "vag," who is, like old Lazarillo, mistreated because he doesn't produce. His labor organizing on behalf of those who produce but still are mistreated has made it impossible for him to segregate space and culture. As he traverses Wyoming he sees first its romantic visage ("a high clean windy state" [139]), then its commodities (coal and phosphate), then its laborers and union organizers. Like many earlier road writers, Kerouac included, he associates landscape with legendary explorers and settlers, but unlike them he passes beyond the historical nostalgia for discovery to the real historical consequences of western settlement. Because the nonfiction road book traditionally casts all but itinerant labor as the "other" condition, one of enslavement, very few move beyond landscape and individual imagination to general discussions of work. The pastoral illusion discourages that move. When, for instance, Daphne Sharp, in *The Better Country* (1928), interrupts her husband's reverie amid the pastoral farms of Kansas to remind him of the pitiful prices farmers receive for their crops, Dallas Sharp replies, "Forget your figures, and let's go by appearances" (60). Most writers of nonfiction road books do; the exceptions, besides Sigal, are Dreiser, Dos Passos (in *State of the Nation*, 1944), all the African American road writers, and, to lesser degrees, Zephine Humphrey and Richard Phenix. Sigal cannot fully reclaim the romance of the road because the road is bound up with capitalistic exploitation and bourgeois conformity. It can no longer signify escape and freedom from either force.

For black road writers, adopting or rejecting the forms and conventions of their predecessors has not always been a matter of choice. For them, the anxiety of race has overshadowed the anxiety of influence. Consider that staple road book prerogative, a new identity. Many white highway writers, perhaps drawing upon both the Romantic idea of plastic subjectivity and the picaresque emphasis on disguise, assume that distance untethers identity: the farther you go from home and work, the more freedom you have to adopt a new self. As Peter Beagle said of traveling in the West, "you could be anything you wanted to be in this land" (107). Black road writers (and John Howard Griffin) have found no such solace in American space. Wherever they go, they find, like Ralph Ellison's Invisible Man, that their identity, insofar as it is determined by others, is fixed. Black road writers share with the chroniclers of vags and Okies and with naturalist writers the knowledge that freedom on the road is not mainly a product of will and space but of privilege bestowed by race and class.

Solvent white drivers may view freedom as merely an escape from responsibility without considering the new economic relationships they establish away from home. For example, they often cease to be producers and become consumers. (Although professional writers may still be "producing" as they go, the point still holds.) By consuming along the road, in restaurants, motels, and service stations, they continue to be productive and so are welcomed. They buy their freedom to come and go unmolested. Indeed, as Warren Belasco has demonstrated, roadside accommodation has since the turn of the century steadily evolved to exclude poor travelers, beginning with the closing of free municipal camps in the early 1920s, when even the unwashed began to get wheels (116). Until a very few years ago, white merchants generally considered black travelers unproductive because they threatened more lucrative white business. The result was an "underground highway" of establishments listed in *Travelguide* (estab. 1946) that welcomed black travelers. Desegregation outlawed the cause of the underground highway, but it did not eliminate its usefulness: only fifteen years ago Chet Fuller was initially refused lodging at a Holiday Inn because he was black (197).

The racial wedge drives deep into road book conventions. White travelers are often alert to charm, atmosphere, and authenticity as they consume along the road. They exercise this unacknowledged privilege by "investing" in establishments that please them. Heat-Moon, for example, gauged eateries by how many calendars hung on the walls—the more the better. When Chet Fuller traveling about the same time ate in a white cafe named Mama's Kitchen in Dawson, Georgia, he did not count calendars. He located all the exits and checked out the people sitting next to them (140). Sometimes the logic of road consuming is turned on its head, as when John A. Williams, having been denied service at a New England restaurant in 1963, found himself carefully "picking out places to stop or, rather, letting them pick me out" (26). A black traveler's money could not purchase the power to enjoy charm or good service or the company of colorful natives. It could not buy him universal access to material freely exploited by white writers. Instead, the black traveler had to be bought, in a manner of speaking, by willing establishments. In the West, a landscape typically celebrated for its power to free the self into space, Williams is even more tightly confined by the constant stares and ridiculing gestures of passing white motorists (96). Even the anonymity granted by the indifference of other drivers—the first prerequisite of Romantic contemplation—is a privilege of race.

In contrast with the "outfitting" and "sanguine departure" segments we have come to expect in road narratives, Williams's leavetaking entails a sterner preparation: "Does a white American have to orient himself psychologically for some aimless wandering about the country? To a degree, yes, but not a great deal. For me some sort of psychological preparation was necessary. Eventually I became ready, but it was a costly process" (viii–ix). When we examine black road narratives later in this study it will become clear that Williams is taking stock of the mental baggage he will carry—the endless mnemonic loop of police harrassment, rude service personnel, glaring pedestrians—as he drives not a "Rocinante" or a "Ghost Dancing" (Heat-Moon) or a "Discovery" (Duncan) but a "vault of safety" protecting him from hostile whites (87).

Black writers also rupture visual surfaces that remain intact for white writers predisposed to nostalgia or pastoral yearnings. Driving south of Louisville, Williams found "the lovely scenery a mocking set behind which even the crimes of Hitler . . . grow pale" (43). Chet Fuller felt "love at first sight" for the "quaint bars and shops like relics from waterfront towns of bygone years" he discovered in Wilmington, North Carolina (84). But he soon had reason to agree with the first black man he talked to there, who reproved him for his judgment: "Beautiful, my ass. . . . Pretty? This is a racist town, brother. . . . It might look pretty from the outside, but it's some nasty shit going down here" (84).

More thoroughly than any abstract criticism, the experiences of African American road writers disclose the economic and social compacts, the unwritten codes of power and privilege, which to a large extent underwrite the "self" of autobiographical American road narratives and affect the judgment of travelers who are more object-oriented than self-oriented. Literary traditions and road book conventions, which condition the eye and shape narrative form and content, are themselves shaped by such forces. These historical pressures are often sublimated in road books by the illusion of displacement—the sense of heightened awareness, disinterestedness, cultural suspension, and control produced by moving away from a place where one feels burdened, confined, and distracted by obligation. The enhanced control of movement and attention afforded by driving seems to suspend the everyday psychic claims of history, claims which fade even more quickly as travelers approach sites where "history" really occurred, back in the gauzy past, and then, like Winifred Dixon's "blood-lust and gold-lust," ceased to be.

Transcontinental driving, especially if undertaken by white drivers, has for these reasons inspired much confident observation and very little honest confusion. The automotive cocoon allows one to be, as Walker Percy's Will Barrett opines, "in the world yet not of the world, sampling the peculiarities of place yet cabined off from the sadness of place" (124). The sadness of a place is its history—its generations, customs, class conflicts, hatreds, beliefs, yearnings—all the entanglements a driver has left behind and would as soon not try to undo somewhere else. For many nonfiction writers the automobile grants intellectual license to ignore these complexities and to exercise instead a kind of glib eclecticism that passes for induction. Sweeping over the land often produces sweeping generalities, inspired perhaps by the repetition of forms, the sheer mass of novel phenomena, the enduring appeal of regional stereotypes, an outsider's eye, and the unlikelihood of rebuttal.

Road fiction sometimes endows the traveler with more elaborate motives and gives place more historical substance. This is the difference between Steinbeck's saga of the Joads and Roland Wild's compassionate but reportorial account of the Okies in *Double-Crossing America*. Just as historical substance can lend context and resonance to travel in *The Grapes of Wrath* or Bobbie Ann Mason's post-Vietnam novel *In Country* (1985), it can be bogus, as in Thomas and Agnes Wilby's *On the Trail to Sunset* (1912), in which the Southwest teems with nefarious "greasers" bent on overthrowing the government. Also, some nonfiction road books, particularly object-centered books like Dos Passos's *State of the Nation*, Ian Frazier's *Great Plains* (1989), and Jonathan Daniels' *A Southerner Discovers the South* (1938), tender very rich historical context. But the fact remains that this context is discerned from an alien vantage. Abstract and dialectical, it can only *evoke* the sadness of place.

Any taxonomy of twentieth-century highway books about America will be troubled by a surfeit of grounds for comparing them. I have mentioned a number of possible rubrics under which they could be grouped: literary mode (naturalism, pastoral, picaresque, satire); theme (self-discovery, escape from bourgeois confinement, racial identity); literary genre (autobiography, fiction, nonfiction, travelogue); persona (picaro, curmudgeon, social citic, troubadour); and tone (nostalgic, bitter, beat, euphoric).

As an example, Dreiser's *A Hoosier Holiday* is a primarily autobiographical travel book comprising several literary modes, dozens of themes, many shadings of a central persona, and a tone that ranges from Olympian detachment to treacly sentiment. Slippery, in other words, like most road books. Dreiser devotes the first half of this lengthy book, which narrates his automobile journey to Indiana from New York with his companion and illustrator, Franklin Booth, to scenic descripton, comments on manners, architecture, and culture, and details of the practical difficulties of the trip. In the second half he wanders his home state from Warsaw to Terre Haute, revisiting the landmarks of his youth. En route to Indiana he presents himself as a cool but tolerant observer, meticulously detailing the charms and foibles of small-town life as well as the bracing energy of industrial cities. The ineluctable pastoral moments of the trip—wayside picnics, skinnydips in country streams—are balanced by Dreiser's distrust of backwater moralism and his admiration for manufacture. He punctuates his observations with Dreiserosophy—a combination of armchair naturalism and social Darwinism that depicts all human activity as an essentially meaningless expression of drives and wills, both of which are perverted by primitive religious codes.

When he returns to his old stomping grounds, the tenor shifts dramatically. The cool, discerning persona gives way to a melancholy voice that is prone to moralize and reminisce. His homecoming all but subverts Dreiserosophy, at least in the sense that Theodore Dreiser, his mother, and all those Hoosiers who touched his young life begin to accrue a sentimental mass out of measure with the significance he has allowed the thousands of people who have slid by his windshield along the way. Yet unlike many later travelers Dreiser does not view his automobile trip as a symbolic journey, a movement that represents a personal metamorphosis. This is neither a Transcendentalist narrative nor a passage narrative but rather a narrative in which place alters perspective but not the whole man. Movement through places that have no personal associations produces object-centered generality, whereas the home ground inspires more subject-centered contemplation—while the narrator sees himself as the same person throughout.

If *Hoosier Holiday* can satirize the yokels on one page, admire their thrift and industry on another, and pity them their brutality on yet another; if it can contain both an elaborate consumer text and a cold Darwinian treatment of labor-management strife, then the search for its kinship with other road books has to begin with broader designs. I think the book fits into three larger categories: the social survey, the rolling philosophical inquiry, and the homecoming. The first includes books that describe, in various combinations, regional manners, speech, architecture, customs, history, myths, culture and so forth, such as Henry James's *The American Scene* (1906), *Double-Crossing America*, *America Day by Day*, *A Southerner Discovers the South*, *Great Plains*, and V. S. Naipaul's *A Turn in the South* (1989). The second connects the events and landscape of the road with a sustained philosophical discussion, often in the form of a dialogue, as between Dreiser and Booth. Other books of this type are Robert Pirsig's *Zen*, Kaj Klitgaard's *Through the American Landscape* (1941), and Jean Baudrillard's *America* (1988). In the last and largest category, the authors return home or to a place where many relations live after years of expatriation to examine changes in themselves and in their old surroundings. Examples include *The Lost Continent*, *South of Freedom*, *This Is My Country Too*, Mort Rosenblum's *Back Home* (1989), and William Saroyan's *Short Drive, Sweet Chariot* (1966).

Hoosier Holiday typifies nonfiction road books that have a male and nondomestic orientation, revivifying the Ishmael/Huck Finn rover who may have male companions but who otherwise looks beyond intimates and family for intellectual fodder. Kin-trip books, in which the narrator's perspective is complicated by other family members who are often in some way along for the journey, run against this grain. Before 1940, most nonfiction transcontinental narratives were in some fashion kintrips, usually involving married couples and often whole families, a trend that died out as such trips ceased to be adventures in themselves and the travelogue gave way to more thematic, or literary, content.[4]

4. In his bibliography of transcontinental nonfiction road narratives up to 1940, Bliss lists twenty-two expeditions that involved either single men or men with male companions, six trips involving either single women or women with female companions, and thirty-seven that from his summaries appear to be kintrips.

At their best, kin-trip books of substance generate novelistic quandries and tensions and occasionally even a complex resolution, as in Nigel and Adam Nicolson's father-son exchanges in *Two Roads to Dodge City* (1987). The Nicolsons, British writers who travel individually but compose letters to one another as they approach Kansas from opposite ends of the nation, manage to crack their mutual reserve and diffidence by critiquing each other's cultural observations, revealing in the bargain the familial roots of their tastes and prejudices. Adam (the son) goes so far as to explain their itineraries and interests in terms of filial rebellion: his father has preferred visiting the "colonnades and structures" of "a great and ordered civilization" in the eastern United States, whereas he has roamed the relatively new West, "bumping around in the froth of bits of individualism," liberated from the class consciousness he associates with his father (203). As they close toward Dodge, their letters grow more intimate, by turns critical and conciliatory, building to a warm but staid reunion in America's mythic capital of frontier violence.

Although the Nicolsons deny us a sentimental climax, they have moved beyond the comparatively practical and incidental family dialogues of earlier kin-trip books like Emily Post's *By Motor to the Golden Gate*, Humphrey's *Green Mountains to Sierras*, and Wild's *Double-Crossing America* to the first full expression of the type since Dallas and Daphne Sharp visited *The Better Country* sixty years earlier. (By contrast, Pirsig's relationship to his son Chris is essentially tutelary, and *Zen*, though technically a kin trip, is by and large monologue.) *Two Roads to Dodge City* introduces familial anxiety—which is often repressed or stigmatized in road books because it constrains the illusory independence granted by the highway—as an aid to reflection, deepening the traveler's sense of his psychic history and how it affects where he goes and what he sees. In so doing, it and other nonfiction kin-trip books approach kin-trip novels such as Sinclair Lewis's *Free Air*, Steinbeck's *Grapes of Wrath*, or Larry McMurtry's *Moving On* (1970) by imposing the guilt, comfort, and duty of family on American space, which we have come to think of as being reserved for the undomesticated author.

The history of the road romance in novels from Thomas and Agnes Wilby's *On the Trail to Sunset* (1912) to Stephen Wright's *Going Native* (1994) generally parallels the popularity and subsequent decline, after the Second World War, of kin-trip nonfiction books. In the Wilbys' novel and Lewis's *Free Air*, the highway tests and tempers lovers, summoning courage and resourcefulness that remain latent in the city, and fosters an arduous but rewarding courtship as the basis for a happy family. After the war, as in the nonfiction books, road trips increasingly depict a rebellion against domestic constraints, and erotic matters have less to do with marriage and children. Kerouac's *On the Road* (1957) retains vestiges of the romance, in that it concludes with nominal marriages, but its energies clearly lie in homosocial flight. In the sixties and seventies Douglas Woolf, Katherine Dunn, and Jim Harrison refine and enlarge antidomestic themes in grim road noir narratives that anticipate the final collapse of the road romance in *Going Native*.

A surprising one-fourth of all nonfiction transcontinental auto narratives produced before the Second World War were written by women.[5] Most of these women, like Zephine Humphrey, traveled America with husbands, but an even half dozen traveled exclusively with other women.[6] In two books of the latter type, Winifred Hawkridge Dixon's *Westward Hoboes: Ups and Downs of Frontier Motoring* (1921) and Beth O'Shea's *A Long Way from Boston* (1946; about a trip made circa 1922), the authors traveled with a single close companion.

Thematically, *Westward Hoboes* and *A Long Way from Boston* have much in common with similar books written by men. For Dixon and O'Shea the auto journey to the far West offers escape from stultifying routine and an opportunity to reclaim a "genuine" self, in Emersonian fashion, from the "layers and layers of other people's personality," as Dixon puts it (274). O'Shea and her friend manage a true picaresque existence, working odd jobs to finance their trip. The vigorous determination of these women

5. Bliss's bibliography shows that fifteen of sixty-five narratives were written by women.

6. Bliss lists seven accounts of women traveling alone or with other women and four other entries indicate possible single-woman journeys.

to surmount the considerable difficulties of the road with wits or brute strength is coupled with understated complaint and a prevailing tone of comic optimism in such a way as to almost discredit the "hazards" that later male writers milk for suspense. To be sure, the self-conscious grit displayed in the books turns as much on gender expectations as it does on personality. These early women road writers understand the novelty quotient of their adventures, and it is primarily this adjustment of their texts to address such expectations that justifies setting apart something like "early women's nonfiction road books" as a category. For example, while neither Dixon nor O'Shea reports any sexual harrassment on the road (O'Shea explicitly says she was never "attacked" [2]), both know that the sexual vulnerability of traveling women is naturally fascinating, and they tease some suspense from awkward sleeping arrangements or rustic bathing. Their transformations into sturdy vagabonds occur gradually, the result of necessity rather than overt rebellion against sex roles, yet they boast of their trousers, their dirty bodies, and their growing mechanical savvy, relishing the inversion their readers expect. Beyond this, both Dixon and O'Shea speak of erotic interests with rare candor, matched only, in my reading, by Dreiser. In all these respects, early women motorists who travel without men distinguish themselves from their finicky white-gloved cousins like Emily Post, who are forever checking the roadhouse linen and shaking out their dusters, and from their fictional counterparts such as Lewis's Claire Boltwood and the Wilbys' Evelyn Deering, who rely on men to deliver them from the perils of the road.

Like most road books, these two fall under several rubrics at once. *A Long Way from Boston* is largely picaresque, and since it relates a young woman's movement from shop-girl servitude to radical independence, also qualifies as a passage story. *Westward Hoboes* features some Transcendental matter and furnishes an early example of cultural ambivalence—simultaneous pride in and suspicion of Anglo conquest—in a sophisticated narrative of rediscovery.

Given the eclectic nature of most nonfiction road books, the value of identifying literary traditions and categories lies not so much in the slots themselves as it does in revealing, first, the power that established forms and types, in league with historical situation and ideological prejudice, exert on the trajectory of road perception, and second, the ease with which such conventions and mental habits are veiled by the road narrative, which often depends for its appeal on the rhetoric of inexhaustible novelty. Penetrating new space calls for fresh perception, what Sal Paradise calls "innocent road eyes" (106) and Jean Baudrillard "the opportunity to be brutally naive" (28). Otherwise, America has already been intellectually consumed, settled, its potential as raw material for the imagination exhausted, unable to supply new places to discover and new symbols for the self.

A parallel yearning for innocence in the material realm has also characterized a good deal of road writing. Until fairly recently, with the rise of environmental concern about the West (strongly voiced in Heat-Moon and Frazier), motoring writers generally ignore the massive and organized incorporation of that region, which was already far along, as Alan Trachtenberg has demonstrated, when the automobile arrived. And although the automobile itself extended and enlarged that incorporation, it continues to enjoy a kind of spiritual exemption. The complaint of some recent highway writers that franchise has destroyed local color always rings a little false, as if cars are as neutral and innocent as thumbs and people ought to stick to their folkways when they drive.

Always qualifying the pattern of regeneration through discovery and self-discovery are writers who tell of the road's victims and refugees and "deep-travel" writers who penetrate pastoral surfaces and the superficies of ethnic and regional stereotype to examine latent economic and cultural tectonics. This division cannot be universally applied, because often the narrative of self-discovery encompasses deep travel and because some deep travelers lapse into triteness or bigotry. Winifred Dixon, for instance, condemns the imposition of Western dress and fundamentalist religion on "dignified" Indians (246), yet she savages Hispanics as ignorant, violent, and lazy (164, 172). In *Hoosier Holiday* the deep-travel curriculum is to some extent reversed. Dreiser renders surfaces—dress, manners, architecture, facial expressions—with brilliant acuity, but when he comes to the troubled sources of production he retreats to a ponderous but consoling vagueness couched as "philosophy." He is not, however, similarly neurotic in his depiction and judgment of surfaces. He seldom settles for the quaint or pastoral impression but in his own version of deep travel looks to religion, ethnic background, and social trends as sources for what he sees. And African American road writers, confronted with inescapable racism, are obliged to travel deeply.

The common thread of highway narratives, from the utilitarian travelogue to the deep travel inquiry to the Emersonian quest, is the belief that America remains a virgin land *for the intellect*. This belief grants the traveler the illusion that he or she can create a new vision of America, reinvent the land, fill in the contours of desire or fear. Having come too late, having already lost to corporations, franchises, and farmers the material power to subjugate labor and resources, auto travelers rhetorically dissociate themselves from this fait accompli and recover America's first promise to the European—an empty place, waiting to be signified by abstractions. The imperialist urge of the recreational motorist may not be Dixon's "blood-lust [or] gold-lust, religion, fanaticism, [or] empire bulding"; but in the highway fiction of suspension and disinterest, in the constant departures and appetite for novelty, we find the yearning for power and superiority undiminished. Automotive Manifest Destiny is an internalized revisiting of the historical fact. The landscape and its inhabitants become the principal American commodity, replacing cattle and coal and hydroelectric power. The labor and machinery required to make the old resources pay in tainted coin are replaced by the nomadic self, which appreciates in value as the innocence or corruption of the land and its people become the traveler's creation, raw material for picaresque adventure, highbrow commentary, and lyrical description.

Implicitly or explicitly, the traveler circumvents the forces of exploitation and production. Innocent of these forces, he or she wields the benign power of transforming landscape and people into objects of entertainment, all the while enlarging and dramatizing the perceiving self. Meanwhile, the machine that enables this process loses its mechanical identity, its connection to labor and environmental exploitation, and becomes a kind of bionic prosthesis, as responsive and potent as remote control.

Sweet Release from the Violent Sleeping Car
and a Chance at Rediscovery

1

The advent of practical cross-country automotive travel in America sparked an immediate back-to-nature trend. Motorists by the hundreds of thousands chucked the routine and comforts of settled life, loaded their cars with lanterns and grills, and went gypsying. One chronicler of this movement, Warren Belasco, explains that autocampers were joining a larger revolt against Victorian institutions when they sought in auto vagabonding a return to the "strenuous life" advocated by Teddy Roosevelt (qtd. in Dixon 360), as well as "alternatives to tiresome gentility," and "immediate experience and gratification that contrasted sharply with the older Victorian production ethic of thrift, sobriety, and postponed satisfaction" (Belasco 107–8). They shunned the railroad as well, that mighty Victorian conqueror of space and time, because it closeted them from nature, subjected them to social constraints, ruled them with timetables, and, worst of all, stank of bananas. Not all early highway writers of nonfiction went into "vagabondage" (Winifed Dixon's nicely ambiguous term), but many of them introduced or interrupted their narratives with an explanation of the sensible differences between rail and automotive travel. These contrasts, developed in sets of opposed images and metaphors, are fashioned to demonstrate the superiority of automobile travel primarily on the grounds that it unbinds and sharpens perception by removing the social and mechanical constraints associated with railroading. These contrasts often veil the similarities between the modes of transportation and even, as we shall see, transpose their attributes.

Among the most commonly mentioned advantages of the automobile over the railroad—one that is also adopted by aficionados of the blue highway—is the intimacy with landscape and people it allows, "the choice, intimate knowledge to which the motorist alone can attain," as Effie Price Gladding put it (ix). Modern railroads, by contrast, move rapidly through a fixed corridor, and the outside world passes in a blur. Lewis Gannett found, in 1934, that the motorcar rekindled the "old intimacies" of mid-nineteenth-century rail travel, intimacies that had been lost in the interim:

> If my father, when I was twelve, had taken me West, we would have ridden in vestibule trains and seen next to nothing of the country. Meals in the dining car; no wayside stops; just the impersonality of a big train or a big hotel. But in 1852, when my grandfather took my father to St. Louis and Chicago, by train and stage and steamboat, the trains stopped at mealtimes to let the passengers eat and at night to let them sleep; and the travellers returned with a real sense of what this country and its people are. The automobile, at last, brings us back to something of the old intimacies. . . . you stop, to talk, to look at a cactus, an eagle or a sunset, to see the sights. (4–5)

In the same vein, Dallas Lore Sharp had earlier characterized train travel as a "violent" experience in that it wrenched the traveler from the continuity of terrain and weather. Automobile travel not only restored this coherence, it joined the contours of mood and land:

> You are close to the earth and the people by motor, an intimate immediate mode of travel, slow or fast to your mood, or the mood of the weather, yet gradual enough, no matter how fast you go, to impress you with the considerable width and variety of the country. . . .

For business the sleeping-car in this country is a necessity; but for real travel it is too utterly violent, the spark of consciousness jumping a five-hundred-mile gap of landscape in a single night. . . . Every mile by motor is a continuous experience. There are no lapses between twilight and dawn. On the train I have closed my eyes in the early dusk of a winter day to a howling prairie blizzard and opened them the next morning . . . climatic zones and geologic aeons apart, a break with the earth so shattering that it can never be mended. . . . It was an end of the road. The bridge of continuity went out in the night. . . . Motoring is liable to violence, Heaven knows, and subject enough to lapses not like those of the "limited train." . . . missing nothing of the road as you do on your flying pillow by train. (31–32)

Sharp's contrasts, emphasizing the earth-hugging intimacy of auto travel, bring to mind Thoreau's comparison of walking and riding the rails in *Walden*, as well as his essay on walking. Indeed Sharp alludes to this essay later in the book, acknowledging that walking is the ideal way to travel, but that motoring, which most nearly approximates the perceptual advantages of walking, provides the only practical choice for a thinking person's transcontinental journey (46). In 1907 Henry James said that the "wonder-working motor-car" enabled him to throw out "the lasso of observation" (48), an expansive cowboy metaphor that finds no comparable moment in his survey of America from a Pullman seat, which he describes as being cramped by a "general pretention" (463). The railroad car, in short, draws the traveler inside, away from the immediate terrain and its inhabitants and into a shuttered, well-appointed nowhere, expedient and comfortable but utterly alien.

Prefacing her account of a transcontinental motor journey from New York to San Francisco in 1919, *It Could Have Been Worse* (1920), Beatrice Massey concluded that driving cross-country was "the only way to get a first-hand knowledge of our country, its people, the scenery" (n.p.). With her head on the flying pillow of a Pullman she would have scudded past the covered wagons of starved-out refugees passing through Montana, missed the "pinched and starved" faces of their children (77), just as ten years later, rail travelers in the West would fly by the abandoned homes of Okies and the procession of their trucks headed to California. For viewing the land, motor travel surpassed rail travel, travelogue, and photography. Massey wrote of the North Dakota Badlands, "You may read of them, see pictures of them, or see them from a train, but you have never really seen their wonder, their grotesquely beautiful grandeur, until you stand in their midst as we did" (74).

The automobile removed the frame from the American high plains and delivered its passengers into the startling desolation that eighteenth-century aesthetic theorists had said inspired the privative sublime—a sense of awe and delightful fear inspired by vast space. Francis Parkman (55–56) and Washington Irving (106) recorded such emotions when they visited the plains in the nineteenth century. Traveling horseback, they, like the automotive apologists who echoed them, were brought to the high plains by conveyances they could walk away from and erase from the scene. Kaj Klitgaard rode in a Ford convertible whose top could be lowered whenever he "wished to feel a part of a scene, as a man on horseback might feel a part of it" (8). That was something one could not do on a train. It warped human scale and too sensibly mastered the landscape, leeching its power to awe and reducing it to a pleasant (or even dull) movie. Later writers often voiced the same complaint about the moving car: its window could become no more than a television screen. The difference between viewing landscape from a train and viewing it from a car, however, was that automobile passengers, unlike rail passengers, could choose not to view the landscape passively.

Winifred Dixon, who gypsied with Katherine Thaxter in the early twenties, complained that "drifting by railroad in the West implies timetables, crowded trains, boudoir-capped matrons, crying babies and the smell of bananas, long waits, and anxiety over reservations." "Traveling by auto," she continued, "seemed luxurious in comparison" (1). Considering the hazards and hardships detailed in her account of western motoring, Dixon's definition of luxury lends a great deal of weight to independence. It is hard to imagine, for example, that fretting about reservations would have created more anxiety than losing one's brakes on a mountain road and descending by crashing the car into the mountainside every hundred feet, as Dixon was forced to do. And timetables surely posed less inconvenience than breakdowns in the desert. Self-containment and self-determination, then, were worth the loss of more secure, reliable transportation—and worth some risk of safety, too.

Dixon and Thaxter entrusted themselves to "a Cadillac Eight, with a rakish hood and matronly tonneau; its front was intimidating, its rear reassuring" (2). Without making too much of Dixon's comic metaphor, for it was conventional to give cars women's features, her repetition of "matron" on adjoining pages emphasizes the difference between being trapped with matrons and their squalling babies on a train and enjoying the security of a matronly automobile, which, by the way, has not lost its sexual vigor. The train is a machine that transports matrons and their banana-eating children, but the car is anthropomorphic, a mother/picara that both nurtures and strikes out on its own.

The complaint that Americans traveling in large groups aboard trains and ships are insufferably alike and insufferably boring did not find its first voice in the disgruntled motorist. In 1842 Dickens had griped about the "deadly, leaden people," "all alike," aboard a western steamboat (204, 215), and a couple of decades later Twain made a running joke of his fellow ship passengers' vexing repetitiousness, bordering on echolalia, in *The Innocents Abroad* (1869). But the motoring writer, it appears, was more likely to stress the claustral nature of rail travel than the boorishness of fellow passengers. Just before the Second World War, Zephine Humphrey explained the spatial basis of automotive freedom:

> When people try to escape from life by setting sail on a ship, they find themselves shut in at close quarters with a lot of other people doing the same thing. When they travel by train, they are still more circumscribed and seem, moreover, to have taken the whole Grand Central Station with them. But when they drive a car, their freedom

is as nearly perfect as possible. Even walking is less emancipating, for the pedestrian often becomes acutely aware of a footsore body. . . . how sweet was our release. The people we [she and her husband] saw did not know us and paid no attention to us; the people we left behind did not know where we were. (17)

Presumably "life" means routine obligations that require social dealings, by their very nature unpleasant. Mass transit destroys the illusion of escape, not only by recreating and compressing social obligations, but by cheating the traveler of her sense of uniqueness. If everyone on a ship or train is escaping too, then her gesture is cheapened by repetition. She has fallen back into routine. More distressing, however, she is denied the freedom to fashion an escape worthy of her self—an escape different from, *and better than*, other people's. To do so requires the "perfect" freedom afforded by distance, which finally severs all connection to routine and society, banishing those other eyes and minds that encroach on perception by threatening to replicate it. Granted anonymity, the motorist can consider herself emancipated, free to create her vision of the continent without competing claims on its singularity.

Humphrey's promotion of automotive travel issues from the Romantic and Transcendental notion that unique and "genuine" perception is enhanced by privacy, if not solitude, flourishing when the press of bureaucracy and convention is left behind. Dreiser's advocacy of driving complements independence with pastoral delights. If, in the mid–nineteenth century, some Transcendentalists viewed the railroad as a path to western nature, Dreiser, in 1916, converted their argument to the blue highway. In so doing he relied on the traditional contrast between the machine and the garden. This opposition lodged the automobile squarely in the garden, where it appears to us still, every day, in hundreds of television ads designed to obscure its mechanical nature and industrial origins. First, Dreiser portrays the railroads as another blighted limb of commerce and industry:

At best the railways have become huge, clumsy, unwieldy affairs. . . .

mass carriers, freight handlers, great hurry conveniences for overbur-
dened commercial minds. . . . smoke, dust, cinders, noise . . . cattle
trains, coal trains, fruit trains, milk trains in endless procession. . . .
our huge railways are becoming so freight logged and trainyard and
train terminal infested, and four tracked and cinder blown, that they
are a nuisance. . . . modern railroading . . . is so fixed; it has no lat-
itude, no elasticity. Who wants to see the same old scenes over and
over? (92–93)

Then he couches the alternative in terms of pastoral independence:

But the prospect of new and varied roads, and of that intimate
contact with woodland silences, grassy slopes, sudden and sheer
vistas at sharp turns, streams not followed by endless lines of cars —
of being able to change your mind and go by this route or that
according to your mood. . . . it appears to make a man independent
and give him a choice of life. . . . only the dull can love sameness. (93)

It seems clear that beyond the simple machine-and-garden contrast lie
richer symbolic implications about driving and the dynamics of production and consumption. Dreiser's language in the first passage transforms
the railroad into an infernal conveyor belt, lugging products from one
place to another through a pall of soot. The repetition of "train" and the
emphasis on the repeated vistas recall the monotonous labor of assembly. I have already noted Dreiser's enthusiasm for the abstract energy of
industry and his dollying back from a labor-management conflict until
it becomes a clashing of abstract forces, neither of which he champions
(379). Despite his appreciation of industrial power, however, he feared
that the Midwest would suffer if industry grew too large there and people were forced to "do dull, routine things" resulting in a "stultifying
world" of "plethora and fixity" (240). The railroad adumbrates such a
world, where people, in this case passengers, are transformed into products to be hauled and purchased by others. Their perception, like Henry
Ford's version of factory labor, is dulled by repetition, alienated from

itself (see Fink). By contrast, driving holds out the pleasures of consuming, choosing among "new and varied" roads as mood dictates. The act of consuming emerges as a sign of independence, whereas producing or distributing signifies fatality and imprisonment. Notice also that as Dreiser's focus shifts from production and distribution to consumption, the commodities change, too. The railroad deals in coal and cattle, fuel and feed, and its proper passengers have gross "commercial minds"; but the driver, ostensibly liberated from the commerce that feeds and fuels him, consumes only beautiful landscape. The automobile becomes the machine that helps him transcend all the other machines.

A similar juxtaposition of machine and garden occurs in *The Better Country*, but with a twist. Sharp's machines are in fact road-building implements, seldom visited in road books: "Unwieldy, uncouth, primordial shapes in steel that bulk like those giant ground sloths, the Gravigrads of the Pleistocene, who . . . uprooted trees with their claws. Machines they are which actually lay down new ribs of rock for the earth" (121). But they are, for Sharp, heroic creations. Metaphorically organic, they reshape a parcel of nature, easing the passage of automobiles into a larger, undisturbed nature where auto gypsies can enjoy the amenities of the train while savoring the freedom of the car: "The ideal motor travel in our wide land is by 'pullmanized auto' (a Kansas City term), and at the first call of the whippoorwill, or at the first faint wash of dusk, to turn into a pasture beside a stream, or into an arroyo, unlimber the frying pan, hang out your tail-light, and be in your sleeping-bag what time the coyotes begin to howl" (123). Thus a rare glimpse of the machines behind the machine discloses a guileless primordial force paving the path to cowboy pastoral.

Even Sharp's broader view of mechanical proliferation in the United States exhibits a kind of wistful fatality that diffuses hesitant and obligatory reservations about the car. He says that "we suffer in our culture" for the great influence of machinery, particularly the car, but Americans "cannot help it" because the automobile issues from our national genius and was inevitable from the founding of the nation (45–46). "What has happened to make the trip by motor from Boston to Santa Barbara so reasonably possible had to happen" (45).

If indeed there was a destiny that shaped our front ends, then according to Sharp its proximate executor, "the Frankenstein," was science, working through "Invention and Big Business" (45). This is a marvelous Romantic conceit—the corporate Frankenstein violating nature by devising a monster that is part human and part machine—but what about the coyotes? What about the "wheels of my being" epiphany Sharp experiences in Kansas? It seems that the Romantic opposition between business-science-machine and leisure-poetry-garden resists integration. Sharp has to deal with one at a time, so he offers his reservations about the automobile in the context of general social criticism while voicing his Romantic response to driving in the more compelling narrative of his own journey. The car's Romantic associations, because they grow out of the central story, finally ease such qualms, which are not so credible if the automobile's genesis was decreed by fate. Sharp's quandary did admit of a resolution, and D. H. Lawrence provided it in 1923 in *Studies in Classic American Literature* (32). *Because* Americans are idealists, Lawrence argued, they build machines to do their work.

Despite the fact that many early transcontinental travelogues, including the first, frankly advertised certain makes of automobiles and parts, it is plain that in many relatively sophisticated American travel books the automobile was, from very early on in its life, dissociated from its economic essence. It was destined to become a mainstay of American manufacturing and service industries, but as a literary creation it was an avatar of distinctly contrary impulses: yearnings for pastoral beauty, individual expression, solitude, freedom, leisure, and contemplation. (Henry Miller alone, among highway writers I read, denounced the automobile in *The Air-Conditioned Nightmare* as a "symbol of falsity and illusion" because it was produced and purchased with "stultifying labor" [33].) The train more or less brought urban, industrial pressures to bear on the activity of travel, denying the solace of an illusory frontier. The automobile reinvented the frontier. As Emily Post said in 1915, "if we overlooked the fact of our own motor car, we could have supposed ourselves crossing the plains in the days of the caravans and stage coaches" (135). In the beginning, mechanical hardships confirmed the motorist's pioneer spirit. With better roads and ubiquitous services, auto travel practically approached the comfort of rail travel. But the urge to deny our industrial economy and discover a surviving preindustrial America in folkways and in Western landscape has proven surprisingly resilient. I view the bulk of American highway literature as an industrial product in the sense that non–Native Americans, always conscious of the space that haunts their history, subject themselves to the rigors of concerted labor in part because the promise of release into pastoral space is renewed in every generation.

The automotive narrative, thoroughly grounded in production and distribution of both cars and books, realizes its opposite condition by fashioning a myth of independence from those forces, and it does so in part by continually reenacting the discovery and early settlement of the country. As Zephine Humphrey put it, "we were not to blame for the fact that we had been born too late to ride in a covered wagon; and, original discovery being no longer possible, it seemed sensible to make the most of a chance at re-discovery. After all, there is a ripeness in re-appropriation" (18).

This reenactment can take many forms. Some motoring authors, like Winifred Dixon and Dayton Duncan, retraced the routes of European or American explorers as they focused on their own experience. Zephine Humphrey likened her transcontinental trip to the westward migrations of Boone, the Mormons, and the forty-niners—hence the term "re-appropriation." William Least Heat-Moon allowed the preindustrial past of America, in particular the doomed visions of Black Elk's Ghost Dancers, to brood over his backroads diatribe against "an enemy future." Other writers were more information-intensive. John T. Faris, in *Roaming American Highways* (1931), sketched genealogies of modern highway routes as he drove them, tracing their ancestry to historical trails like the salt river road and El Camino Real (95). In a more desultory fashion John R. Humphreys visited *The Lost Towns and Roads of America* (1961), gleaning historical lore to feed the nostalgic imagination. Ian Frazier's *Great*

Plains, the most focused and deftly composed of these info-narratives, shuttles back and forth through time, visiting and revisiting the discovery and settlement of the Great Plains in different historical contexts so that the promise of rediscovery, while rich in the West's surviving spaces, always involves the consequences of the original venture.

More commonly, the rediscovery theme does not govern the entire narrative but is prompted by an evocative feature of the landscape—Donner Pass being a grim favorite. At its most casual the theme may appear abruptly, without much resonance. For instance Grace Hegger Lewis, accompanying her husband Sinclair on a 1916 four-month gypsying tour that provided material for *Free Air*, called their trip a "voyage of discovery": "Crossing the great Missouri from Bismarck to Mandan . . . we were Lewis and Clark!" (99, 101). The Wilbys, around the same time, played the same enthusiastic riff about Independence:

> The Santa Fe Trail! The automotive traveler of to-day needs but to don the magic spectacles of imagination to transform the scudding car into a huge bird on whose wings he is borne into the romantic land of dreams and historic memories. No longer the attractive "suburb" of a modern Kansas City, but a quaint group of sheds and rough log-houses for the trappers of the wild, surrounding country. (127)

The landscape near Platte, Nebraska, awakened in Dallas Lore Sharp visions of

> the creaking caravan, the tepees on the flats, the thunder of wild hoofs upon the prairie, and the whoops of hunters on the flanks of the shaggy herds.
> We had entered a new world. . . . Here were the lights and the bare boards of the stage and much of the scenery, but the actors in the stirring drama, so swiftly borne away! (84–85).

Or the theme may be enlarged to accommodate that familiar union of romance and social criticism that peoples a lapsed America with heroic ghosts. Kerouac's ardor for the road is a yearning for novel and elemental experience denied by the repetition and hierarchical abstractions of bourgeois life. The road mystically connects Sal Paradise with his preindustrial counterparts, Daniel Boone (who "promised to find the Gap") and the "men who whooped her up in log cabins" (105), as he recovers their freedom vicariously. But when past and present intersect, the here-and-now makes a feeble show, reversing the Wilbys' progressive bent. Passing through Council Bluffs on his way west, Sal wistfully notes the erosion of this frontier gateway by bleak modern settlement: "All winter I'd been reading of the great wagon parties that held council there before hitting the Oregon and Santa Fe trails; and of course now it was only cute suburban cottages of one damn kind and another, all laid out in the dismal gray dawn" (19).

During Henry Miller's Parisian sojourn, as related in *Tropic of Cancer* (1961), he tempered his disgust for American culture with some nostalgia for its striking landscapes (208). Returning for the transcontinental car trip that would yield *The Air-Conditioned Nightmare*, he sustained that divided judgment, echoing Henry James and Dickens in decrying the ugliness and crass commercialism of America while celebrating its natural beauty. In fact, Dickens and Miller shared the hope that the blighted civilization erected by European immigrants would soon collapse and the continent revert to its primitive state, which would again be ruled by Indians (*American Notes* 205 ff., *Nightmare* 229). In a passage remarkably like Kerouac's, Miller works an historical split screen as he crests Cajon Pass on his way into San Bernardino:

> Everything but the ocean seems jammed into this mile-high circus at sixty miles an hour. It wasn't I who got the thrill—it was a man inside me trying to recapture the imagined thrill of the pioneers who came through this pass on foot and on horseback. Seated in an automobile, hemmed in by a horde of Sunday afternoon maniacs, one can't possibly experience the emotion which such a scene should produce in the human breast. (245)

Though there are moments in *The Air-Conditioned Nightmare* when

Miller takes a grudging interest in his car, as he does in the comic "Automotive Passacaglia" chapter, as a rule he finds it a kind of necessary evil, something to help him rediscover the bayous and desertscapes he relishes but otherwise a drag on his imagination.

Also among road books in which the rediscovery theme is adjunct to larger designs, Sigal's *Going Away* treats the frontier as a state of mind, reflecting the narrator's early confidence in the unbounded possibilities of his future and his subsequent confusion and despair as he learns that American culture, with its domestic and commercial fetters, has voided the promise of its landscape by stifling the individual freedom that landscape once prefigured. When the narrator went AWOL in 1946, he fled west

> in a rush; beyond the Mississippi was a new vastness to him as exciting and potential of adventure (perhaps even a lucky stroke of salvation) as it had once looked to Marquette and Pike and Fremont and Big Bill Haywood. Westerly he went, on the fringes of the first lap of the wave that was to carry back whole demographic chunks of America to the Rockies, to the Pacific, away from the known and old and tried to the new that was already (though none knew it) turning tarnished, the truly last frontier turning green at the edges before anyone could lay a firm hand on it. (97)

In the ten years that pass before he launches his expatriation in a transcontinental drive eastward, he witnesses the progress of this "tarnish" in Los Angeles—not only overpopulation and suburban isolation, but an ethnic jumble tenuously held together by a false and sentimental idea of community. Though still an advocate of organized labor, despite his realization that its cause is doomed, Sigal's narrator has also learned out West that he cannot himself tolerate repetitive labor and that his attachment to the cause has been in some ways artificial and disingenuous. A two-year stint in the Hollywood dream factory completes his alienation, and as a literal substitute for pistol and bullet, he takes to the wilderness road, which now signifies retreat and introversion. The pioneers' ghosts have not vanished, but their function has changed. Whereas once he looked on the wilderness through their eyes, now, on his anguished easterly excursion punctuated by psychotic episodes, he internalizes these figures, with whom he holds long conversations as he drives. Near Donner Pass he talks to the Donner children and warns their parents of the tragedy to come (138–39); farther on he converses with Lewis and Clark, Jim Bridger, and Chief Joseph of the Nez Percé (168). But these dialogues are now furtive and hesitantly acknowledged, symptoms of the narrator's depression. They do not augur a healing Romantic vision of the West but instead signal the collapse of Thoreauvian individualism in bourgeois America.

Sigal has authored one of the darkest road passages in the subjective mode, chronicling the disintegration of a self-conscious wayfarer who exhausts the recuperative powers of the western highway and fulfills Tocqeville's direst predictions for the American thrown back entirely on himself in American space. *Going Away* offers few palliatives. Its narrator is painfully honest but often unsympathetic. His angst barely redeems his self-pity; his goading of friends en route is downright invidious; and his ambivalence toward women, who seem to be either fetching earth-mothers-at-the-end-of-the-trail or soul-snuffing housewives, reminds one of Leslie Fiedler's complaint that American male writers have long been unable to imagine complex and companionable women characters. And yet it is hard to discount the weight of his broken ideals for America, his loneliness and sadness flung across the landscape — strains of Melville's dark Romanticism in *Moby-Dick* and *Pierre*, of the Beats' existential fatigue. Coupled with his refusal to erase modern labor from the terrain, these responses challenge the blithe historical imaginations of many road writers before and after Sigal who window-shop the West.

Sigal's novel cannot be faulted for its narrator's despair; that is the condition Sigal imagined for his protagonist. Were *Going Away* a work of nonfiction, however (and it may in fact be close to that), we would expect that the narrator's alienation be shown to have some clearer connection to the rediscovered frontier, that all the cultural shams he flees arise either from the seeds of westward expansion or in opposition to it, and that the poverty of choices he bemoans does not in fact grow from a petulant longing for Western anarchy.

When the rediscovery theme enters a road narrative, it usually means, as the old novelist quipped, an Increase in Seriousness. It signals a departure from merely practical and visual matters—the literal journey—and a move toward temporal context and comparison, toward symbolic possibilities. It is less likely to appear in road books that smudge the road experience and foreground the local operation of government and business. Such books, among them *A Southerner Discovers the South*, *State of the Nation*, and *American Journey* (none of which deals with the far West), generally concentrate on specific struggles between people who have power—managers, bureaucrats, labor leaders and politicians—and people who don't, usually workers. Because, in these books, the traveler is supposed to be an objective observer whose feelings and subjective impressions count for less than his reportorial judgment, they seldom tender Romantic or mythic notions by way of explanation. Such impulses are more characteristic of *spatial* works, with at least some Western content, that give more rein to imagination.

Returning now to books in which the rediscovery motif is more sustained than incidental, I find that in some cases the "historical dimension" is merely the second dimension. Rediscovery books like Dixon's *Westward Hoboes*, Faris's *Roaming American Highways*, and Humphreys' *Lost Towns and Roads of America* are "flat" in the sense that they do not seriously probe either the personal or social implications of the historical information provided along the way. They elicit instead the reassurance of imagining a quaint Disney past, of "peopling the road, successively, with Indians, colonists, Quaker traders, English soldiers" (Faris 17) while journeying "as though by time machine from one living American Brigadoon to another" (Humphreys 14). John Humphreys' simile tells all. The automobile is like a time machine in which one is seated to watch American history on parade: a succession of romantic musicals, perhaps—lilting and scrubbed, with an MDR of nostalgia and not an ounce of causation or guilt. Or maybe a film festival: "The road also leads to places only the imagination knows, raised for us out of fiction and the silver screen of a dark movie house" (Humphreys 189). And if you catch the right film, you might see a rendition of John Faris's charming Florida roadside attraction: "The road is lined with [the negroes'] little cabins, where, so often, windows are not needed . . . and there, in the evening, the members of the family gather for the rolicking ending of a care-free day" (145). Winifred Dixon's earlier book, which also featured an historical itinerary for the "modern pioneer" intent on discovering "the old movie life of the frontier" (3–4), exhibits only fleeting moments of cultural self-consciousness, as when Dixon and her companion Thaxter sense the absurdity of fundamentalist proselytizing in a Hopi village (246). Otherwise she professes to be a disinterested adventurer, thus distinguishing herself from the "resolute men" whose paths she retraces (90). Though neutral in deed, Dixon is anything but neutral in word. She is enchanted by the heroic exploits of Coronado but has nothing but contempt for his "lazy" and "ignorant" descendants, among them the Penitentes of northern New Mexico. Members of this very old and clandestine order of flagellants, according to Dixon, shrive themselves at Easter and "during the rest of the year commit murder, adultery, theft, and arson with cheerful abandon" (171–72). She does not say how a lazy race can manage such havoc.

Spectator, tourist, satisfied customer: these are such books' implied readers, whose rediscovery amounts to a kind of *post facto* consumer imperialism. Labor and class, racial conquest and exploitation are expunged from the map or relegated to the distant past, and their absence is itself a reassurance and a comfort that such nasty work has already been done by someone dead and gone, leaving the continent a myth emporium for travelers who seek, as Dixon put it, "the romance of a thousand years."

Revisionist stirrings appeared fairly early in the history of automobile narratives, though my reading suggests that qualms about the course of empire were uncommon before midcentury, perhaps because the closing of the frontier was so recent. And when such early misgivings were expressed, they were likely to be timid queries. Even so, challenges like those of Dallas Lore Sharp and Zephine Humphrey were precocious. Though Sharp short-circuited some of his social criticism by falling back on a bogus historical determinism, he did not hesitate to affirm, in 1928, that "killing, robbing, hounding, jailing, and pauperizing the Indian has been one of the noble occupations of our democratic Government" as has been "this forcing upon him of an alien, mechanistic, materialistic education" (118).

Humphrey scooped the quincentennial revisionist attacks on Christopher Columbus by fifty years, asking in 1936, "To the American continent did the year 1492 seem a glorious date?" (36). In the introduction to *Green Mountains to Sierras*, Humphrey tried to strike a balance between veneration and censure of America's past:

> But what national heritage is anywhere richer in romance than that of the United States? Not long since dead and buried either, but so recently over-past that it still stirs and beckons, still admonishes. . . . for it is founded on something deeper and stronger than our politics. And, since the proud civilization with which we have veneered the ancient land is beginning to wear shabby and thin nowadays, it may be that a latent wisdom will presently shine forth. (21)

The message here is ambiguous. Humphrey might mean that the failures that are part of America's national heritage will admonish its modern citizens to act more wisely. Or perhaps she is suggesting that the pioneers and settlers were possessed of transcendent motives to which modern Americans should return in hopes of rescuing the nation from its maladies. The historical subtext of her automobile narrative supports the first interpretation. Her journey through the "black blasted realms" of Allegheny coal country revealed the human cost of an industrial society and reminded her of other workers whose labor made her trip possible (21). In Oklahoma the "ugly and noisome" oil wells were "blighting the earth and polluting the air," causing her to wonder "whether the end is noble enough to justify the means," and the sad history of Indian removal to that state convinced her that "Uncle Sam has shown himself neither a generous patron nor a good sport" (53). Crossing the Texas panhandle, she passed "the queer caravans" of the Okies' "rattle-trap motor cars" (60). Farther west, in Taos, she came to reverence the ecological thrift of the Pueblo Indian and "winced and burned at the revelations of high-handed spoliations on the part of the white man. Treachery too, and cruelty. . . . it took all my faith in the purposeful wisdom of destiny to withstand my increasing sorrow that Christopher Columbus should ever have been born!" (120).

By the time Humphrey delivers her conclusion, this meliorism, which begins to support the second interpretation of her introduction, no longer requires such an effort, and the accumulated evidence of cultural and ecological wrongdoing vanishes. It vanishes because in the end her own migration by car has led her to identify with her predecessors so that she comes to feel she has a stake in Manifest Destiny. Here she and her husband pass through the Cumberland Gap:

> Thoughts of Daniel Boone crowded upon us; and, the better to arrange our historical associations as well as enjoy the beauty of the place, we alighted the top of the pass. . . . we realized what an impassable barrier it must have seemed to the early settlers until, guided by Boone, they dared the adventure of penetrating through the Cumberland Gap. Not much of a trek was it when compared with the Mormon migration, or the vicissitudes of the Forty-Niners, or the earlier Spanish explorations, but in the same historic tradition, part of the same historic heritage. Returning from the West to the East, we found our sense of historic values immensely quickened, and our faith renewed. Surely a people with such a brave experience in its blood can be trusted to perfect a stalwart civilization. (243-44)

The "historic values" Humphrey invokes are vaporous at best, and might better be called by her own term, "historical associations." The values she used to judge, in the course of her journey, the human and environmental consequences of American expansionism and industrial development have come into play whenever she has witnessed something that irritates her faith in the benevolence of American destiny. The automobile, with its vaunted power to grant intimacy, has brought her up close to such problems and forced her to acknowledge them. But it has also sped her away from them, and they have diminished into the sweep of space. Coursing across the continent in an automobile is an experience that verges on pure abstraction, and Humphrey seizes on the largest of our history's spatial patterns and its repetition though time (including her own automotive age) as the embodiment of America's destiny. Humphrey's "destiny," much like Sharp's, admits no values. And it nullifies the local and the personal.

Humphrey's capitulation to such a romantic vision of the past and future is disappointing. Yet *Green Mountains to Sierras* raised signal questions about America's mythic past and its bearing on a dubious present and future—questions that Miller and Sigal intermittently addressed and answered differently. In 1961 Sigal said that "America's past in the West was never romantic, but that's no reason to spit on it" (167). This is the baseline sentiment for later nonfiction road books that incorporate the rediscovery topos, the most prominent of which are Heat-Moon's *Blue Highways*, Dayton Duncan's *Out West*, and Ian Frazier's *Great Plains*. These books combined older road book conventions with secularized but deeply ambivalent notions of the past they were reappropriating. Firmly in place are the lighting-out-for-the-territory motif, the backroad strategy (as old as Dreiser), pastoral oppositions, and the claim of intimacy (subdued in Frazier).

Thematically, the discontent with quietistic suburbia voiced in Kerouac's and Sigal's road writing merged, in these later books, with the country's broader and more thoroughgoing popular interrogation of American history during and after Vietnam. Heat-Moon, Duncan, and Frazier were writing in the wake of popular revisionist histories, novels, and movies about the West, which exposed in particular the brutal treatment of western Native Americans and which began to nurture a counterromanticism similar to but more enlightened than nineteenth-century elegies for the "children of nature."[1] And it goes without saying that the Civil Rights movement had laid bare the drastic consequences of a rationalized exploitation that for centuries had driven the cultivation of the South.

Another revolution, in our ideas about American nature, left its mark on these books. As symbolically profound as the closing of the frontier in 1890, the environmental alarms raised in the sixties and seventies dramatically shrank the continent by making it seem more fragile and vulnerable—susceptible to biological exhaustion brought on by a host of modern assaults, from auto emissions and salt-laden fertilizers to acid rain and strip-mining. The tally of our depredations mounted rapidly in the decades preceding these books, and their authors were tasked with inventing new terms for the automotive rediscovery.

The main problem was how to sustain the romance of historical associations and spatial liberty while acknowledging the sins of the fathers. When the sin in question was the decimation of western Native Americans in the 1800s, all three authors addressed the problem in similar fashion. They cultivated an informed sympathy for the western tribes by providing many details of tribal histories, rituals, and customs, and by chronicling the devastation these tribes had suffered at the hands of military and civilian agents. Sometimes, as in certain segments of *Blue Highways*, this sympathy verges on mystical identity as Heat-Moon, part Sioux himself, invokes Black Elk; but in general the details of Native Americans' lives flesh out and humanize the conquered peoples so that

1. For example, revisionist histories include *The Red Man in the New World Drama* (1971), by Jennings C. Wise, rev. by Vine Deloria, and *North American Indians in Historical Perspective* (1971), ed. by Eleanor Burke Leacock and Nancy Oestreich Lurie. Also see Trachtenberg's *The Incorporation of America* (1982). Thomas Berger's novel *Little Big Man* (1964) was made into a movie by the same name in 1970 by director Arthur Penn. The films *Soldier Blue*, directed by Ralph Nelson, and *A Man Called Horse*, directed by Elliot Silverstein, also appeared in 1970.

the Indian presence in the Old West can become part of these travelers' romantic historical associations without the condescension that marred earlier narratives by Post, Dixon, the Wilbys, Wild, and many others.

When the sin was ecocide, the romance of historical associations proved much handier. Predictably, the operant conflict pitted government and big business against rude nature, stewarded by Native Americans, or cultivated nature, stewarded by family farmers, a few of them Native Americans. On the road the traveler seeks vestiges of prelapsarian America, the unmarred landscape that appears as it did to natives and explorers or small farms such as those plowed by early settlers. At other times he motors east of Eden to visit the grim monuments of progress: Interstate highways, franchise restaurants, hydroelectric dams, strip mines, and smelters. This is what might be called the historic pastoral, the stark, symbolized opposition of natural and technological forces over time, and it operates with a Manichean simplicity that throttles any serious opposition, much less debate, about its worth as a model. About its usefulness to highway writers there can be little doubt. Above all, the historic pastoral enhances the established pastoral affiliation of the automobile because the car is the rural seat of observation and contemplation, the vantage from which the traveler can view despoiling industry and pristine nature. The automobile's connections to those turbines and smelters are soft-pedaled, if not ignored.

This pastoral opposition is also auspicious to road books that emphasize road experiences—"horizontal" books, as opposed to "vertical" travel books like Dos Passos's *State of the Nation*, which downplay the travel itself and dwell instead on the knotty particulars of some local conflict—because such an opposition addresses environmental ethics with a symbol set of visual surfaces and chance encounters with people. This shorthand, more pronounced in Heat-Moon and Duncan than in Frazier, suits the pace of horizontal narratives, which require a quick turnover in impressions, but it usually fails to produce a considered and coherent environmental vision that takes into account the automobile culture itself.

No road book I have read has balanced a Romantic emphasis on highway experience with a painstaking inquiry into local economy. The emphases seem to be mutually unfriendly.

Heat-Moon's salient achievement in the best-selling *Blue Highways* lies apart from its popular appeal as a Romantic or nostalgic adventure book in the rediscovery vein. He set a high standard, by which highway books will be judged for decades to come, in the lyrical, image-thicketed prose of his nature writing and Transcendental argument (chapter 3). In *Blue Highways* the rediscovery motif is usually tied to this neo-Transcendental process of self-discovery, and both themes generate elevated, sometimes hyperbolic, expression. This straining for significance is caused, in the rediscovery motif, by the sheer ordinariness of a camper trip through late-twentieth-century America. Blue roads or not, the hazards Heat-Moon faced were nothing beside the flash-flooded arroyos, rock slides, and precipitous stage roads that motorists seventy years before had tossed off with strained nonchalance as inconveniences. Indeed, the history of road narratives by white drivers clearly shows that the amount of suspense in the text is inversely proportional to real danger on the road. Because traveling and self-discovery are linked in *Blue Highways*, Heat-Moon's flight from a lost job and a broken marriage must find a symbolic expression with enough solemnity to raise his gesture above pique— to dramatize, if not mythicize, his personal crisis. Sigal and Pirsig had succeeded with similar strategies, so Heat-Moon, with his crustiness up to their example, launched his journey with much ado about rediscovery.

First there is the outfitting. He describes his converted van, lists his spartan provisions, and counts his money (9). The obvious Transcendental connection, also discussed in chapter 3, is with Thoreau's spare but detailed catalogue of building material, supplies, and cash on hand at the beginning of his experiment at Walden Pond. A little farther back, Lewis and Clark inventoried their hardware and foodstuffs for future readers of their journals, which Heat-Moon bought on his trip (240). In the highway book tradition, provisioning is an old convention, really a more useful part of the text in the early days when motorists and aspiring "transcontinentalists" who read them could not drop into Sears for supplies along the way.[2] In 1915 Emily Post enlisted her butler, Edwards, to pack such things as African water buckets and blocks and tackle (12–14). True to form, she named among her favorite portables a silk bag and a tube of pheasant paté. Heat-Moon's closer models were Steinbeck and Pirsig, neither of whom had much truck with silk bags. Steinbeck's appointment of his camper, "Rocinante," in *Travels with Charley* (1962), was strictly utilitarian. But Pirsig's lengthy and subdivided list of gear and tools in *Zen* was meant to set the stage for his encomia on austerity and the "classical" understanding of machinery (34–37).

Heat-Moon doesn't yammer on about his outfitting, but he makes sure we understand that his needs and his equipment are simple, in accord with the Native American–mystic side of his traveling persona. If we don't get the message, he unloads on a "3-BR-splitfoyer" Airstream as an example of what Americans will buy when they want to "get away from it all while hauling it all along" (225). Materially, this is a matter of degree (a bicyclist could level the same shot at Heat-Moon), but the Romantic plasticity of the motor vehicle as a literary symbol makes it more manifestation than machine. If your motives are pure, so is your car. If your persona is a thrifty Transcendentalist, then what you drive is not a Recreational Vehicle, but a small, austerely furnished van, "self-contained but not self-containing" (9).

Two "pasts" are revisited in *Blue Highways*. The first is an ancestral Plains Indian past, which is revived in the imagination. The second is the surviving past—folk atavisms and other pockets of resistance to modern mass culture. The frontier into which Heat-Moon ventures is anyplace off the beaten path, anyplace where vestiges of preindustrial folkways survive. These two pasts correspond roughly to two historical groundswells of nostalgia in America. Christopher Lasch characterizes the first, which occurred in the mid-1800s, as an expression of "genteel primitivism": regret for the loss of the West and its noble natives to settlement, a regret voiced by wealthy, disinterested residents of the

2. For example, see O'Shea (13–14) and Wild (16–17).

Northeast (92–97). According to historian Peter Clecak, whom Lasch cites, the second "nostalgia boom," which roughly coincided with the publication of *Blue Highways*, was a "clinging to the social past" as a refuge from anxieties created by the transition from industrial to postindustrial culture (Lasch 117). Alvin Toffler describes the Left's version of this nostalgia as being based on "bucolic romanticism" and an "exaggerated contempt for science and technology" (qtd. in Lasch 117). While Heat-Moon isn't interested in developing a coherent political vision from this nostalgia, but rather a personal vision, or "harmony" (224), in which the past has symbolic value, Toffler's description generally fits the dilemma Heat-Moon superimposes on modern America.

The Native American past, more specifically the final Sioux Ghost Dances inspired by futile visions of Indian reclamation, broods over the book from Heat-Moon's first night on the road—when he "wrestled memories of the Indian wars"—as a judgment on a botched European culture, the "enemy future" of the continent (7). In his peregrine meditations, he conflates the decimation of the Plains Indians and the subsequent obliteration of regional folkways by commercial icons and specialized labor. He draws sparingly but pointedly from Black Elk's account (edited by John Neihardt) of the Ghost Dances. These dances, which took place in the 1880s and ended with the massacre at Wounded Knee in 1890, were inspired by the visions of Wovoka, a Paiute holy man in Nevada. Wovoka told several Sioux emissaries that he had seen "another world coming. It would come in a whirlwind out of the west and would crush out everything in this world, which was old and dying. In that other world," all dead Indians would be alive, the bison would flourish, and the Wasichus (white men) would disappear (Neihardt 233–35). The Ghost Dance prescribed by Wovoka, through its blend of vision and natural harmony, would dispel the hunger and subjection of the Sioux and restore the ecological balance undone by Anglo expansion. It would also demonstrate the power of magic rooted in nature over abstract materialism and its concomitant exploitation of nature.

The surviving past, which Heat-Moon explores in his van, "Ghost

Dancing," is threatened by franchise restaurants (16), Interstate highways (10), and (in Louisiana) the Corps of Engineers (127, 240). The revived past has already been destroyed by such forces. In either case the past is more or less hidden, "authentic," pastoral, and provincial, while the present and future are blatant, counterfeit, commercial, and national.

In *Blue Highways* the act of rediscovery is itself bound up in a binary rhetoric. Since the "enemy future" (281) is built on conformity, routine, and security, the traveler who seeks to skirt it must "chuck routine. Live the real jeopardy of circumstance" (3), endure "dislocation and disrupted custom" (295). To be fair, beyond relating a few police hassles and some miserable camping episodes, Heat-Moon doesn't press his hardships unduly, but the gesture—part Beat, part Thoreau, and part pioneer—feels mannered, however fit. One has only to think of the Joads, or even Kerouac, to see how far Heat-Moon's "real jeopardy" is from real jeopardy on the road. Strip away this hyperbole, and, materially, you have a vacation in an RV. The difference lies in the sensibility of the traveler, which is nostalgic and Transcendental, putatively ascetic but clearly in many respects bourgeois. The transcontinental jags in *On the Road* are similar experiments, but Kerouac and company, in their brushes with beatness, travel much closer to the edge. Their lyrical and mystical ramblings reveal a desperate expediency, and their struck-up friendships link them with the desperately poor. Kerouac's persona, Sal Paradise, must survive on his vision, compensate for hunger and cold with poetry. In this way, Kerouac goes on the road as a tramp and, sometimes, an outlaw; he stands more radically outside the mainstream than Heat-Moon. His material situation accords more believably with his traveling posture.

Heat-Moon's Thoreauvian shrewdness allows him a sort of genteel poverty on the road. He occupies a middle ground between destitution and superfluity, which affords him independence within the limits of respectability. He can stand, rhetorically, outside the "Interstate" culture, with its blind shuttling and its stultifying reproduction of services and images, by becoming, in RV parlance, self-contained. And herein lies one of the paradoxes of the book: self-containment, which is supposed to give the individual a standing point outside a declining culture, implicates him in the most basic follies of the enemy future: considerable waste, self-indulgence, and an insatiable quest for novelty.

When Heat-Moon, as a modern "explorer," visits the past, he is implicitly dissociated from the forces that have violated it. Here the older past of *Blue Highways* is excavated to rebuke the present:

> At North Bonneville, the first of the immense dams that the Corps of Engineers has built on the Columbia at about fifty-mile intervals, thereby turning one of the greatest rivers of the hemisphere into staircase lakes buzzing with outboards. Unlike the lower river, Lewis and Clark would not recognize the Columbia above Bonneville. Rapids and falls where Indians once speared fish lay under sedimented muck; sandbars and chutes, whirlpools, eddies, and sucks were gone, and the turmoil of waters—current against stone—that ancient voice of the river, silenced.
>
> There was, of course, a new voice: the rumble of dynamos. (240)

The historical pastoral supplies a complete and closed symbol set: modern machines—outboards and dynamos—have buried the garden Lewis and Clark surveyed and Indians tended. If the garden has not been perverted by machines, the traveler can savor a perfect recovery of the explorer's first encounter. One such visitation of the surviving past in *Blue Highways* finds Heat-Moon at the headwaters of the Mississippi, in Minnesota:

> I had knelt to taste a stream coming from a dark, slick lake leaking spirals of mist. In a narrow strip of sky opening above the brook, a great blue heron somehow got its bulk airborne without snaring immense wings and long dangling legs in the close mesh of branches. The lake was Itasca and the stream, a twelve-inch-deep rush of cold clarity over humps of boulders, was the Mississippi River.... [Henry Rowe] Schoolcraft—led by the Chippewa, Yellow Head—traced the Mississippi to Itasca. . . . He recorded in his log that the area was

full of "voracious, long-billed, dyspeptic mosquitoes". . . . A century and a half later, the dark timber still sounded with their whine. (293)

Reminiscent of Dreiser's "woodland silences" passage and Sigal's Massachusetts epiphany, though more fluent and detailed, Heat-Moon's homage to Itasca adds historical association to intensify the pastoral. Much as Humphrey had invoked Boone on her passage through the Cumberland Gap as a way of apotheosizing her journey and joining it to the general myth of Manifest Destiny, Heat-Moon in both passages introduces the European-American explorer as a witness to the virgin land, one whose enviable gaze the latter-day explorer tries to recover. When the landscape has been marred and the gaze is irrecoverable, as is the case with the lower Columbia, then the fantasy of possession can't be imaginatively shared, because nature has already been physically mastered; thus the response is elegiac and, out of frustration, censorious. But when the explorer's vantage remains intact, as it does at Itasca, the modern imagination can stake its claim to fallow land.

One of Heat-Moon's recurring complaints in *Blue Highways* is that modern mass culture devours local community by replacing folkways with media- and business-fashioned images and goods. In other words, community, where it still exists, is threatened primarily by those forces that straighten out the highways and build hydroelectric dams. Yet his own historical vision, which is egocentric, does not adequately involve the historical tie between community and technology in modern America. He views them as antagonistic forces. For Heat-Moon community is an ideal, a Whitmanesque abstraction (garnered from far-flung encounters) that holds the same appeal to him as vestiges of the frontier. And if one lodges the authenticity of the self entirely in its whimsical imaginative independence, then history becomes much more the force that satisfies or checks desire (in this case a yearning for wilderness or folk culture) and much less a complicated, impersonal dialectic of interests that shape community and occasionally touch the individual. The Native American element of Heat-Moon's persona not only links him to the lost pastoral, it gives this monolithic idea of the enemy future a kind of historical cachet, which in turn reinforces another side of his persona, the intellectual vagabond. The automobile journey merely exaggerates this sort of historical view, for the driver is sequestered yet constantly regarding fresh surfaces. The images he takes in, if his is a horizontal trip, tend to become emblems, symbolic tableaux—seen, described, imaginatively transformed, interpreted, and deposited in the order of the narrative. Moreover, in Romantic fashion their reference is primarily to the self. At the simplest level, hydroelectric dams and superhighways are bad because they obstruct the mental pleasures of the pastoral ideal and by extension threaten the self nurtured by American wilderness.

Almost necessarily *Blue Highways*, like most road books, represses the industrial and commercial bases of its production. To name a few: oil wells, refineries, and tankers for the thousand gallons of gasoline powering "Ghost Dancer"; mines, smelters, forges, glass plants, tire plants, and the Ford assembly plant that made the van; a large stand of loblolly pines and a paper mill belching sulphur dioxide fumes to make the pages of the book; offset presses; the climate-controlled offices and commuting editors of Little, Brown; semitrailer trucks ferrying boxes of books over Interstate highways; hundreds of well-lit and air-conditioned bookstores; and finally mega-kilowatts of electricity, generated by coal, nuclear fission, and, yes, hydroelectric dams, to power this machinery. The automotive and publishing industries are not bucolic enterprises, but they thrive in part on the business of reproducing the American pastoral ideal for every industrial generation, just as Catholicism built in Carnival, an inversion of its discipline, to make its rigors more tolerable. I am not suggesting that Heat-Moon is a hypocrite, or that his lyrical musings and deft character sketches ought never to have found a mass audience. But the combination of individualism and nostalgia in *Blue Highways*, because it lacks the economic dimension of earlier books like *State of the Nation* and *A Southerner Discovers the South*, whose authors brought no overriding romanticism to their examinations of colliding agrarian and industrial forces, actually perpetuates a kind of wistful fatalism that embraces the pastoral myth and concedes its inevitable loss.

Dayton Duncan's *Out West*, published five years later, was the amiable and plainspoken son of *Blue Highways*. As I have noted, Duncan frankly appropriated many of Heat-Moon's devices, including an elaborate dissertation on cafe triage (106–8). But *Out West* lacks the craftsmanship, the seasoned contemplative strain, the mysticism, and the melancholic—sometimes caustic—spirit of Heat-Moon's book. It occasionally suffers from too little discrimination in incident, which bogs the narrative. Still, it is a good-humored and unpretentious book, honest in its derivations and at ease with its casual delivery.

Duncan took for his itinerary the route of Jefferson's Corps of Discovery, and he duly named his borrowed Volkswagen van "Discovery." From the outset he merges the familiar backroads creed with his program of rediscovery, thereby invoking the two pasts of *Blue Highways*. Although Duncan's revival of prelapsarian America shares with Heat-Moon's the basic design of the historical pastoral, including frequent contrasts between the virgin land encountered by Lewis and Clark and the mechanically transmogrified landscape of the modern West, he dispenses with Heat-Moon's brooding mysticism, opting instead for homiletics, a smattering of sentiment, and some forced solemnity. Likewise, the surviving past in *Out West*, while still presented as an assortment of fetching characters and colorful slackwaters, does not bear so much symbolic weight. Briefly, Duncan's book is not so Romantic, in the literary sense: it is more object-centered and less subject-centered than *Blue Highways*, though on a continuum it has more to do with the traveler than a book like Ian Frazier's *Great Plains*. Moments of self-examination are rare and affected, but personal experience (in the I-did-this-I-did-that format) dominates the narrative.

In Duncan's book the decline of the West is still recorded by a combination of historical fact and existing artifact, but it is not a personal affront or a symbolic ingredient in a private mythology. Duncan's objective bent, however, fails to yield an historical vision any more intricate than Heat-Moon's, though both, as I have said, address the impact of Anglo settlement on Native Americans with more sensitivity and knowledge than their roving predecessors. Facts about the Lewis and Clark expedition accumulate, as do vistas ruined by technology, all without much discrimination among the forms and motives of ecological exploitation. The absolute costs are, of course, indisputable. Duncan reads the grim roll of ecological outrages (e.g.,77) and disease and despair on contemporary reservations (97), citing the clash of two views of nature, one "harmonizing," one "intent on conquest" (167). Always, the latter is depicted in mechanical terms—"the machine of white civilization" (167), "the machine of Manifest Destiny" (104). More specifically, the Great Falls of the Missouri, "the grandest sight Lewis ever beheld[,] has been turned into kilowatts" (225); "the location of the principal Mandan village during the explorers' time [is] now under a powerplant and a coal slagheap" (187).

The mechanical and conquest metaphors, though on the mark, once again deflect attention from a recreational slate that reproduces the conquest impulse and mechanical means while implicitly claiming exemption and historical distance. Dixon's avowed innocence of the "blood-lust and gold-lust, religion, fanaticism, and empire building" of earlier travelers is reborn in Duncan's Road Rule 10: "The theology of the road forms its own religion, combining bits and pieces of other beliefs. It relies on technology (a vehicle), yet respects the forces of nature. Its deity is the Road Spirit; its principal practice is the pilgrimage" (140). This is an egregious case of having it both ways. If the spirit of reenacting discovery is heightened by car trouble (355), one winter night spent in an earthen Hidatsu lodge (182), and an encounter with a snow-clogged pass; if, as Duncan claims, massive RVs verify Tocqueville's judgment that Americans are singleminded in their pursuit of material wealth (340), while a vw camper betokens austerity, then Duncan is surely playing symbolism against culpability in his desire to cloak himself in the innocence of the first explorers.

A few years before Duncan went out West, Italian author Umberto Eco undertook an American journey to explore the condition of "hyper-reality," a term he used to describe the effect of historical facsimile in such places as the Hearst Castle and Disneyland. Eco observed that "for historical information to be absorbed [by Americans], it has to assume the aspect of a reincarnation," a "full-scale authentic copy" that purports to be the real thing but is actually "the absolute fake" (6–9). This demand for facsimile is part of "the constant 'past-izing' process carried out by American civilization in its alternate process of futuristic planning and nostalgic remorse" (9–10), and it stems as well from "the unhappy awareness of a present without depth" (31). Eco put fresh spin on the complaint voiced by travelers from Henry James to Baudrillard that Americans cannot properly view themselves as living in the stream of history because they ignore or reinvent the past. While Duncan certainly cannot be accused of completely ignoring history or of turning the West into a scrubbed and guilt-free precinct of Disney World—indeed his is a much more culturally sensitive perspective than that of most travelers before the 1960s—his narrative does rely a good deal on the simulacra of expedition and the historical isolation of region and era. In the larger scheme of *Out West* this objectification, part of which takes the form of the historical pastoral, amounts to the "reincarnation" Eco speaks of: both the vestiges of the frontier and the emblems of its demise are frozen and suspended, while the spectator, assuming (sometimes ironically) a frontier guise, complements the illusion. In this case the facsimile incorporates the sins of the fathers and the visitation of those sins on the sons and daughters, but it still puts space between the spectator and the "machine of white civilization." The motoring traveler's imagination thus plays over static forms, reducing stubborn and very hard problems of history to the operation of sinister mechanical forces.

Most white "horizontal" road writers with any social conscience at all skirt the quandaries that arise when the automobile becomes a medium for viewing the evidence of social ills. Just as the car has impoverished our inner cities by enabling wealthier citizens to claim a parcel of the bucolic suburbs and shirk rather than confront the urban problems they created by leaving, in highway narratives the automobile always deadens the impact of blight and misery because it promises escape to the pastoral alternative. Thus environmental and human injuries come to be seen as spatial rather than historical phenomena, as existing rather than evolving. This effect is compounded by the fact that the automobile can always produce the frontier simply by ferrying its driver away from settlement and industry. In sum, the automobile is justly celebrated for its power to tap "the romance of a thousand years"—to convey us to the landscapes of our historical mythology—but at the same time, it fosters the illusion of historical and moral detachment and neutrality.

In the early going of his distinguished *Great Plains* Ian Frazier advances a metaphor that is reminiscent of Eco's hyperreality: "The Great Plains have plenty of room for the past. Often as I drove around, I felt as if I were in an enormous time park" (82). And in good retro-pastoral trim Frazier goes on to describe the incursion of technology into the park:

> Like other arid but inhabited parts of the world, the plains some-times hold pieces of the past intact and out of time, so that a romantic or curious person can walk into an abandoned house and get a whiff of June 1933, or can look at a sagebrush ridge and imagine dinosaurs wading through a marsh. In the presence of strip-mined land, these humble flights fall to the ground. Scrambled in the waste heaps, the dinosaur vertebrae drift in chaos with the sandstone metate, the .45–70 rifle cartridge, the Styrofoam cup. It is impossible to imagine a Cheyenne war party coming out of the canyon, because the canyon is gone. . . . Of a place where the imagination could move at will backward and even forward through time, strip-mining creates a kind of time prison. (90–91)

Once again the point of reference is the disinterested individual in the present. Relatively undisturbed nature offers him a parklike setting in which he can "re-appropriate" (to use Humphrey's term once more) the

West; nature scarred by technology claps him in an imaginative prison because it denies him the reenactment of naive exploration.

Let me be clear. I do not for a moment champion the indiscriminate strip-mining of coal in the West. Frazier builds a moving and worthy case for the preservation of the Great Plains, a region that is particularly susceptible to exploitation because it appears to be a wasteland. My argument is not with the environmental idealism of such travelers, but with the implicit disavowal of technology and industry in the absence of a larger frame of historical and social reference—a specious rhetorical independence of technology that haunts these modern road narratives and compromises their insights. The historical pastoral is instructive but finally disjunct if it is not jolted out of its mental situation.

A related impulse in *Great Plains* is what a friend of mine who lived near the Navajo reservation in New Mexico called "yearning": Anglos who hang around the rez and long to exchange their repellant Western ways for the "wholeness" of Navajo culture are called "yearners." Frazier does not exhibit all the symptoms of a yearner, but in a book largely devoted to stories that do not involve the narrator, the rare personal moments usually tell of his excitement in the presence of those shoved aside in the course of American history. An example is his sojourn in the largely African American town of Nicodemus, Kansas:

> Suddenly I felt a joy so strong it almost knocked me down. It came up my spine and settled on my head like a warm cap and filled my eyes with tears. . . . And I thought, *It could have worked!* This democracy, this land of freedom and equality and the pursuit of happiness—it could have worked! . . . It didn't have to turn into a greedy free-for-all! We didn't have to make a mess of it and the continent and ourselves! . . . the sight of so many black people here on the blue-eyed Great Plains was like a cool drink of water. . . . For a moment I could imagine the past rewritten, wars unfought, the buffalo and Indians undestroyed, the prairie unplundered. Maybe history did not absolutely have to turn out the way it did. . . . I was no longer

a consumer, a rate payer, a tenant, a card holder, a motorist. I was home. (173–75)

It is cold-hearted to say so in the glow of such a tender and winning moment, but I can think of no better example of an automotive shriving than this personal climax of *Great Plains*, which brings Humphrey's reluctant faith in Manifest Destiny half circle. It groans with the weight of perfectly reasonable cultural guilt. All the pastoral oppositions are firmly in place, and the automobile has brought its driver within reach of an idyl whose surfaces betoken the surviving Other living in apparent harmony. The traveler is whisked out of the nightmare of time and guilt and into a *place* where he need not feel guilty, because the victims of his culture have literally found a home on the range—and Frazier quotes Brewster Higley's song to prove it.

"Sampling the peculiarities of place yet cabined off from the sadness of place." We might go Percy's phrase one better and say "idealizing the peculiarities of place." I am homing in on this spatial fallacy in Frazier to illustrate a pattern among modern road books—to show an ahistorical impulse being expressed in the midst of a densely historical text—but I would be shortchanging a rich and delightful book were I to leave it at that.

In its merging of journey and Western history *Great Plains* extends the possibilities of both the regional history, like Walter Prescott Webb's classic book *The Great Plains*, and the highway info-narrative such as *Roaming American Highways* or Jill Schneider's *Route 66 across New Mexico* (1991). Unlike Heat-Moon or Duncan, Frazier did not build his book around a single journey (Duncan combined two into one), so it is not, generally speaking, a horizontal narrative. Instead, he drew his road experience, garnered from several summers' driving, into a discursive sequence of topical narratives and quasi-essays. Robert Bly once referred to his own associative brand of verse as "leaping poetry"; Frazier's method is something like leaping stories. His road material establishes place as a personal experience, evocative in its smell or artifacts or weather—

not for Transcendental ends, but as a catalyst for historical, botanical, or climatic digression. Meandering and backtracking associations lead away from the immediate road experience, forward and backward through time and space, creating a raconteur's collage of the Great Plains. This approach is cartographically represented in two facing frontispiece maps, one depicting crossings of the Great Plains by Coronado, Lewis and Clark, Pike, Long, and Parkman, and the other Frazier's convoluted wanderings over the same region. One by one, Frazier's narratives and discussions of immigration patterns, wheat varieties, plant introductions and migrations, and soil conservation techniques are swept into the vortices of places on the road, until the plains landscape becomes a vast swirl of failure, chance, and invention. As a native of the Great Plains and one who has driven many thousands of miles on its roads, I find in such digressions, unburdened by the Manicheanism of the historical pastoral, a much more instructive depiction of surfaces as palpable registers, in the present, of human action in the past, because they trace a resident population and its *evolving* impact on an environment, for good or ill, instead of reducing environmental questions to a modern false dilemma of abstract alternatives.

On the other hand, historical celebrities, whose exploits are writ large in *Great Plains*, have virtually nothing to do with the anthropology of surfaces viewed by the modern motorist. In some cases, as with Crazy Horse, Sitting Bull, and Custer, such figures embody opposed sets of cultural values; in other cases, as with Bonnie and Clyde, Bob Wills, or Lawrence Welk, Frazier situates the circumstances of their fame in the landscape of the Great Plains. But of course the overriding appeal of stories about historical celebrities lies in the power of individual fame to subjugate place and transform it into a romanticized backdrop for human action. For the automotive traveler, this kind of imaginative flight differs from both the rediscovery scenario (by extension the historical pastoral), in which the emphasis remains on the virgin land itself as the desirable object of an explorer's gaze, and the Transcendental impulse, in which landscape and solitude enhance self-awareness. The traveler seeking the "authentic" situation of an historical celebrity—a battleground or birthplace—participates to some degree in the quest for hyperreality, except that hyperreality is a "hot" condition requiring little imaginative participation, whereas the haunts of historical celebrities are relatively "cold"—incomplete facsimiles.

Making their escape from the violent sleeping car, automotive travel writers and some novelists exploited the versatility of a new machine to imaginatively recreate the conditions of frontier exploration and conquest. The solitude and independence of motor travel were auspicious to this fantasy, which Zephine Humphrey called "re-appropriation." The imperialistic connotations of that word finally hold for Humphrey, who ultimately embraced Manifest Destiny as a transcendent force and explicitly connected her own motor trip with the conquest of the frontier. In general the metaphorical opposition of machine and garden, which Leo Marx traced through the history of nineteenth-century American literature, continued to operate in highway narratives after 1900. With the glaring exception of Henry Miller, most highway writers of nonfiction did not burden the automobile with the insidious associations traditionally reserved, in this opposition, for technology, choosing instead to celebrate its power to remove us from technology's industrial nightmares in the Northeast and return us to the garden of the American frontier. So the general pattern of the nonfiction narratives is an escape from confinement in work, often in northeastern cities, and a release into western pastoral space, where it is possible, imaginatively, to recover both the virgin land of preindustrial America and the experience of having that land all to yourself, of projectively mastering it. Urban twentieth-century America bore too many palpable reminders that the machine had finished the promise of individual freedom predicated on space, and the automobile, by granting private access to the remotest tracts of the country, provided a consoling reversionist fantasy. Almost literary in its power to offer up the landscape of desire to a solitary imagination, the car, as a kind of perceptual prosthesis, erased its own mechanical identity and along with it the whole system of production and distribution that lay behind it, even as it erased, for drivers before midcentury, the pervasiveness of technological systems in the West.

While the automobile remained an "innocent" machine in more recent road writing, keener environmental awareness after the 1960s, coupled with heightened sensitivity to the continuing plight of western Native Americans displaced by European expansion in the nineteenth century, complicated the rediscovery theme, leading recent highway writers to alter the reversionist fantasy by incorporating extensive and sympathetic treatments of Native American cultures, and by condemning the irreversible alteration of landscape by power and mineral interests. In the latter case writers often employed what I have called the historical pastoral, a symbolic contrast, related in an elegiac tone, between a pristine preindustrial setting (often as described by early explorers) and some industrial eyesore that has obliterated it. The laudable environmental sentiments bound up in the historical pastoral are sometimes compromised by Manichean and egocentric historical prejudices. In any case, after 1970 it was hard for any serious road writer to undertake the rediscovery program while viewing the conquest of the West as a benign process.

A Hammock of Supreme Indifference:
Highway Consciousness

2

When early road writers like Dreiser made a case for the automobile as a better means of seeing America than the railroad, they emphasized its ability to afford intimacy with nature and obey the whims and moods of the traveler while freeing him or her from the social constraints of rail travel. On the road, the objective world comprised the forms of nature more often than the forms of society; as the social claims faded, driving itself exacted claims on the new subjective freedom by making stiff demands on motor skills. Many early highway writers, including Dreiser and Post, were chauffeured. Those who were not must have been too consumed with practical things to muse on the driver's split consciousness, for digressions on this topic don't seem to have amounted to much until the thirties, when road conditions had generally improved enough to allow drivers considerably more time for reflection. When, for instance, the heroine of Sinclair Lewis's *Free Air* (1919) encountered a common stretch of bad road near Gopher Prairie, Minnesota, "she was too appallingly busy to be frightened, or to be Miss Claire Boltwood, or to comfort her uneasy father. She had to drive. Her frail graceful arms put into it a vicious vigor that was genius. . . . She fought the steering wheel as though she were shadow-boxing" (4). Forty years later, Steinbeck remarked about driving that "nearly all reactions have become automatic.

One does not think about what to do. Nearly all the driving technique is buried in a machine-like unconscious. This being so, a large area of the conscious mind is left free for thinking" (*Travels* 94). Provided, of course, the roads are paved.

The highway interface has inspired in the accounts of later writers various and even contrary descriptions of road consciousness, those states and angles of mind peculiar to the reflective driver. I have always admired the candor of the morbid or neurotic driver whose defensive driving amounts to waylaying the imagination before it ruins the trip. Steinbeck did not avoid expressways only because they violated the blue highway code. He found that without the stimulation of secondary roads, too much of the conscious mind was left free for pondering regrets (95). In the late thirties Roland Wild was dismayed to find that on "lonely stretches of road, I had a return of a complaint that has always affected me, and which is common, I believe, among long-distance motorists. I get to thinking of the worst possible accident that can happen, and the miraculous fact that it has not" (103). Boredom is just a little less painful. Michael Robertson occupied himself in the desert by letting his eyes range "over the instruments on the dashboard, checking the gas, the temperature, the mileage and clock" (137). Oblivion is better still. Simone de Beauvoir said that driving induced a "happy stupor"—no less happy, one imagines, for the martinis she downed at rest stops (131), and Richard Phenix felt "cradled in a hammock of supreme indifference" (64). Heat-Moon complained of "highway hypnosis" that made him sit "blindly, dumbly like a veiled stone sphinx" (280). And Jean Baudrillard called driving "a spectacular form of amnesia" (9).

The Romantic or Transcendental interaction between subject and object is blocked in such moods by monotony and withdrawal, resulting from an awareness that the machine has overcome nature and is holding it at a distance. The pleasure that Beauvoir and Phenix speak of is the white noise and security of the womb, granted by the same comfort in the machine's mastery. To describe this sort of perceptual passivity, road writers have often adopted cinematic or televisual metaphors, which cast the driver as a spectator viewing the landscape on the windshield screen. In most cases the medium is "warm" in the sense that it requires little imagination on the viewer's part. The Scottish ex-POW Robertson, writing in the late forties, confessed to wanting to hurtle through the desert, a tendency he had formerly held against Americans: "I made no real contact with the desert, as I bowled along the great highway in the ease and comfort of my car. I might just as well have been viewing it on the screen, from the stalls of a moviehouse" (159). Robert Pirsig, whose machine was of course a motorcycle, argued that the automobile by its very construction induced this perceptual lethargy: "In a car you're always in a compartment, and because you're used to it you don't realize that through that car window everything you see is just more TV. You're a passive observer and it is all moving by you boringly in a frame" (4). Baudrillard thought that tourism—unreflective travel—was best undertaken in the desert, which could be "seen televisually" as an unintrusive backdrop (8). Heat-Moon considered this idleness of mind a temporary lapse. He once caught himself chortling at a tourist snapping photographs from her car when he himself "was rolling effortlessly along, turning the windshield into a movie screen" (194).

In every case the traveler resists the charm of aesthetic distance created by the pleasantly alienating distortion of speed, not only because spectating is passive, but also because it reverses the roles of the writer (who creates and assembles scenarios) and the reader (who spectates). The travel writer cannot surrender his verbal mediation to an inferior and visual medium that is prone to induce complacency by reproducing stock images instead of creating fresh and challenging ones. He makes a point of his resistance—yet another device, like the picaresque posture, in the rhetoric of highway writing—in order to elevate his discourse, and to reassure us that his intellect, not his car, controls the narrative. Once again, the automobile must remain, rhetorically, a neutral device, a tool in the service of an independent mind. If by the rhetorical trope *ekphrasis* the writer can first show how the automobile takes on the qualities and powers of a mass medium, like television or cinema, and then resist its appeal in that form, he can distance himself from the vulgar use of the car as a medium of passive entertainment, though he might abuse it as happily as any other driver.

Kaj Klitgaard, a Danish American artist (who was, to be fair, chauffeured), did not consider the aesthetic distance created by car travel a drawback at all. Indeed his urbane and witty *Through the American Landscape* turns on the framing metaphor. Klitgaard twice crossed the continent for the purpose of viewing each region "in terms of artists who have spent their lives learning to understand and to express in paint the moods of those various landscapes" (218). Along the way, he filtered roadside landscape through the stylistic lenses of American landscape painters, some whose work he already knew and some whose work he was discovering in collections around the country, in order to see the "symbols" (as he called stylized renderings of natural forms) these painters had attributed to landscape that in many cases had never been painted before. In Texas, for example, he looked for Tom Lea landscapes; in New Mexico those of Andrew Dasburg. Reproductions of these artists' works appear in place of the conventional place photographs as a sort of parallel visual complement to the narrative.

Even so stout a program was not at all times proof against cinematic or at least photographic passivity. As he motored through the deserts and mountains and seashore of California Klitgaard admitted that his "reactions to the surroundings were more those of a moving picture camera registering form and color on a strip of celluloid" (213). He began to think in photographic rather than painterly terms—imagining camera placement took the place of recalling painterly symbols—because the landscape beggared stylistic manner. He was unaccountably compelled to frame the scape instead of searching for its latent abstract forms. Though Klitgaard conceded that there was some energy and vision lost in this transition, he did not consider the photographic impulse a completely deadening one, for the framing itself was an exercise in composition.

Not surprisingly, as a book written by a painter with a literary bent, *Through the American Landscape* contains some very fine road writing about motoring perception. Klitgaard adopted the metaphor of a moving dome, somewhat in the manner of Shelley's "dome of many-coloured glass" in "Adonais," to define the limits of his field of vision. Instead of merely occurring in space, objects and the ambient atmosphere are said to appear on the dome, in relation to one another, as if in a hemispherical frame: "Showers were falling from different black patches on the dome" (182). Aesthetic perception of the *immediate* roadside, he discovered in conversation with his sometime fellow-traveler Henry Mattson, another painter, is altered by speed so that objects lose detail but assume bolder abstract form. In a rolling dialogue early in the book Mattson convinced Klitgaard that the "time element," or "speed," was essential to modern painting:

> [Mattson:] "Did you see that tree?"
> "Yes."
> "Did you see how many branches it had?"
> "—"
> "You didn't. You just saw it had branches. Now, when [Maurice de] Vlaminck paints a landscape, he puts in a tree, like this, a stroke." Henry Mattson drew a line on the windshield in imitation of Vlaminck painting a tree. "Then he puts in more strokes—branches—and there is his tree, and in that manner he has put into his painting: *Speeeed*. That's what I mean by speed in painting. We might be as conscientious about our work as the old masters and spend as much time on a canvas—but we can't use their symbols. People are going too fast to read them." (22)

Thereafter, on his road trip, Klitgaard regarded the blurred forms of objects he passed—road signs, filling stations, advertisements—as testaments to the "relativity" Mattson had attributed to modern art. In a sense this insight offers an aesthetic and perceptual alternative to the complaint, going back at least as far as Thoreau in American literature and reiterated in the tv-screen passages, that mechanical locomotion can alienate passengers from nature by effacing detail. Klitgaard suggests that speed offers us a novel aesthetic perspective, the same way squinting or donning Claude-glasses recasts natural forms as painterly symbols.

The effects of highway speed on perception also fascinated Jean Baudrillard, a French traveler who discussed them at some length in *Amerique* (1986), translated as *America* (1988). Baudrillard looked to read American culture through both the process of driving and the landscape of the desert Southwest, a speculative program that yielded some pointed interpretation and many dubious impressions. Since mobility and space have come to be the most familiar distinguishing qualities of America for so many foreign visitors, Baudrillard's plan to begin his extrapolation there naturally suffered from built-in preconceptions, notably the supposed causal connections between space, speed, and cultural superficiality. A society that rapidly consumes surfaces, the argument goes, in turn loses its power to interpret them. Space then becomes "the very form of thought" (16), and the collective consciousness becomes "brutally naive" (28), severed from history and territory. Most Americans are in fact like the tourist who looks at scenery—and, by extension, all phenomena—televisually or cinematically and sees nothing more than a montage of images, without context, so that "mobility or the screen" takes precedence over reality (55). Baudrillard's observations are contemporary variations on familiar themes broached by earlier travelers such as Tocqueville, Frances Trollope, Henry James, and Frederick Jackson Turner. The automobile, television, and cinema are introduced as new mechanical means of reproducing or even exaggerating the effects of continental space—"astral" or "sidereal" space (*sidérale*, 5)—which suggests that there is in *America* something of Dallas Sharp's fatalism about the development of the automobile: even the machines Americans exploit are inevitable responses to their lavish space.

Baudrillard wants to go in two directions simultaneously with his musings on space. The first is the analogy between the superficiality of driving and the superficiality of American culture; the second is an attempt to divorce "astral" space from "the deep America of mores and mentalities" (5) as a way of acknowledging the limits of the analogy. In this rather contradictory scheme, the act of driving sometimes illuminates American mores and mentalities and at other times prompts a more personal consideration of automotive phenomenology:

> you have to take to the road, to that travelling which achieved what [Paul] Virilio calls the aesthetics of disappearance.[³]
>
> For the mental desert form expands before your very eyes, and this is the purified form of social desertification. Disaffection finds its pure form in the barrenness of speed. All that is cold and dead in desertification or social enucleation rediscovers its contemplative form here in the heat of the desert. Here in the transversality of the desert and the irony of geology, the transpolitical finds its generic, mental space. The inhumanity of our ulterior, asocial, superficial world immediately finds its aesthetic form here, its ecstatic form. For the desert is simply that: an ecstatic critique of culture, an ecstatic form of disappearance. . . . Speed creates pure objects. It is itself a pure object, since it cancels out the ground and territorial reference-points, since it runs ahead of time to annul time itself, since it moves more quickly than its own cause and obliterates that cause by outstripping it. Speed is the triumph of effect over cause, the triumph of instantaneity over time as depth, the triumph of the surface and pure objectivity over the profundity of desire. . . . Triumph of forgetting over memory, an uncultivated intoxication. . . . Driving like this produces a kind of invisibility, transparency, or transversality in things, simply by emptying them out. It is a sort of slow-motion suicide, death by an extenuation of forms—the delectable form of their disappearance. . . . Speed is simply the rite that initiates us

3. In *The Vision Machine* (1994) Virilio argues that "with *topographical memory*, one could speak of *generations of vision*, and even of visual heredity from one generation to the next. The advent of the logistics of perception and its renewed vectors for delocalizing geometric optics [as for instance viewing landscape from a moving car], on the contrary, ushered in a eugenics of sight, a preemptive abortion of the diversity of mental images, of the swarm of image-beings being doomed to remain unborn, no longer to see the light of day anywhere" (12). Baudrillard refers explicitly to Virilio's *Esthetique de la disparition* (1980).

into emptiness: a nostalgic desire for forms to revert to immobility, concealed beneath the very intensification of their mobility. (5–7)

It has been commonplace in the history of road narratives for travelers to remark a feeling of "utter insignificance," as one fictional character put it, in the deserts of the West (Wilby 273). Usually this feeling is pleasant, as it is for Baudrillard, because it shrinks one's feelings of guilt and responsibility. The desert, according to Michael Robertson, is "raw cleanness and purity." It "resolve[s] all complex things into simple, basic matter" (156).

Beyond echoing these conventional responses, Baudrillard, in the free-wheeling abstract Franco-jive we have come to expect in the late twentieth century, describes a self-conscious perceiving akin to Shelley's in "Mont Blanc" with speed as a new variable. In that great Romantic lyric, the poet's confidence in an organic interchange of powers between mind and nature wavered on the "Remote, serene, and inaccessible . . . naked countenance of earth" in the French Alps (2:97–98). Mont Blanc raised the specter of an alien, inscrutable Nature whose forms, while suscepti-ble to human interpretation, might be empty of inherent meaning, like the "pasteboard mask" of natural forms that infuriated Melville's Captain Ahab. Baudrillard's modern version lacks the anxiety and commotion of the old Romantic treatments; as a sophisticated post-Darwinian man he seems to take the process of his own disaffection and disappearance in stride. Speed intensifies the otherness or outerness of nature perceived through the windshield—turns its forms into pure objects—by renewing the surface too quickly for any of the usual conscious adjustments to it to kick in. The automobile passenger loses "territorial reference points" and memory of the immediate landscape, so his ability to contextualize and interpret the land is short-circuited by an excess of surfaces. I am reminded of Bruce Chatwin's tale of the Aboriginal man, Limpy, who, accustomed to navigate the outback on foot by following the phrases of a memorized terrain-song, when taken aboard a truck tried to speed up the song until it turned to gibberish (291–92). Speed creates pure objectivity, according to Baudrillard (following Virilio), by multiplying objects faster than memory can grasp them, so fast that the eye takes up the next image before imagination or memory (subjectivity) can work on one that has just passed. When the surface is transformed by speed, then speed itself becomes the object, because the landscape can't be seen except as a product of speed. The car is naturalized, invisible, part of the self and culture that are disappearing into the speed-forms.

Baudrillard shares with Klitgaard and Mattson the notion of relativity in driving perception, but Klitgaard and Mattson keep personal aesthetic subjectivity at the core of the process, translating speed-altered features into symbols that remain connected to an artistic tradition. Baudrillard suggests that driving in the spaces of the American West sunders cultural connections by leeching out the subjective potential of the landscape, creating pure objects that defy any cultural interpretation but still in some way define culture by signifying its absence.

The opposite—interior and subjective—extreme of highway consciousness is similarly enabled by the car's being "obliterated" by speed, as Baudrillard put it. Once the effect has hidden its cause, the aesthete or philosopher may look outward or inward indifferently, with the scudding landscape a given. The motoring ruminations of William Saroyan in *Short Drive, Sweet Chariot* sometimes touch conventional pastoral delights, but they also at times exemplify a profound withdrawal in the presence of landscape—a withdrawal not into oblivion but into healthy auto-analysis that takes place in pleasant natural surroundings:

> Psychiatry of one sort or another is what happens on a long drive. It has *got* to happen, even if the driver is alone. Memory unburdens itself to that side of himself which is the great listener, and every man *has* that side—he's *got* to have it. Part of the machinery in man, in the mystery of him, is this listening personality, this willing listener to everything. Until the arrival of Freud, every man's built-in listener was the only psychiatrist, and his help constituted the only effective practice of psychiatry. This listener has been given many names, some

of them by Freud: super-ego, id, alter-ego, and so on. By Jung it has been called the collective memory. . . . Certainly the best healing is the healing which comes from God, or from the whole complex which is beyond comprehension. And there is surely nobody who at any time is entirely exempt from a need to be healed.

The Americans have found the healing of God in a variety of things, the most pleasant of which is probably automobile drives. (42–43)

If Henry Miller is the Calvinist of American driving and Heat-Moon the Transcendentalist, Saroyan, with his blend of pocketbook analysis and can-do mysticism, must be the Unitarian Universalist. This is a rare argument for automotive therapy that is not finally anchored in what lies outside the car. Instead of a portable rural seat, the car becomes more like the old *hortus conclusus*, an enclosed garden or secluded retreat originally conducive to religious meditation but now a place for secular introspection. The vestige of piety in Saroyan's diction—the heightening of purpose—links his digression with otherwise diverse road attitudes (epiphanic pastoralism, neo-Transcendentalism, quasi-mystical phenomenology) and sets it apart from more mundane dispositions (neurosis, indifference, passivity, boredom) that are unsuitable because they undermine the subversive, prophetic, or investigative purposes espoused in most highway narratives. The banality and tedium of driving must be repressed or reproached in the literary depiction of driving consciousness when driving is the central signifying act, discovery the central purpose, and nonconformity the salient posture. When the general truth about driving awareness is allowed, it takes the form of confession, general resistance, or satire.

Transcendental Motoring

3

"Everything good is on the highway," Emerson argued in his 1844 essay "Experience" (480). He meant that a robust intellect required the sounds of common speech, the scenes of commerce, the social leveling, and the natural vistas afforded by the road in order to test and temper ideas born in solitude. The highway was for Emerson a symbol of how experience complements idealism when the solitary mind engages with nature and other people. His philosophical program, set forth in *Nature* (1836), is based on transcendental reason, a faculty that orders and shapes what we experience, whose operation had been explained by Immanuel Kant in his *Critique of Pure Reason* (1781).

Nature is a difficult treatise in which Emerson tried to discern the relative contributions of mind and nature in the act of perception. Transcendental reason provides our only access to nature, everything that is not in the mind. We cannot know nature except through the medium of reason. Nature, however, aids reason by supplying it with basic physical properties, such as unity and division, condensation and diffusion. Nature also grounds and enriches language, which suffers when it is wrenched from its roots, as for instance when the word "currency" dies as a metaphor and comes to denote only "money." When reason and nature enjoy a wholesome reciprocity, the earnest perceiver who becomes aware of their mutual influences rises above a merely utilitarian view of nature, transcends objective reality, and experiences a mystical union of self and ultimate reality.

Emerson's application of these ideas in essays such as "The American Scholar" and "Self-Reliance" has won him a much larger forum than *Nature* could ever have done, and the essays have had a greater impact on road writers. But the even more practical demonstration of Transcendentalist notions by Henry David Thoreau in *Walden* has proven the stoutest legacy of the New England Romantics. This curmudgeonly iconoclast taught by example the virtues of simplicity, thrift, and nonconformity. He demonstrated that intellect had been imbruted by excess labor and numbing routine, that the potential of reason and imagination was being spent in a wholly exploitative consumption of nature. The remedy to these spiritual ills, Thoreau argued, lay in material frugality and intellectual vigor. As Emerson had said, the secret of moral and spiritual renewal was in self-reliance—a refusal to conform for the sake of conforming and a new faith in one's own judgments and intuition. The imagination, according to both Thoreau and Emerson, could be liberated as an active, shaping power if it were not harnessed by convention and stupified by labor. An immersion in unspoiled nature would enliven both imagination and language and clarify the spirit.

Walt Whitman, whose *Leaves of Grass* expanded from a small book in 1855 to a weighty tome in 1892, tested Transcendental ideas on a much wider range of human experience. Adopting the persona of a sanguine vagabond—a picaresque poet—he cast himself not as a Jeremiah or a moralist, but as a companion. This persona takes us far from the New England of Emerson and Thoreau to the streets of New York City, the paths of the Old Northwest, the swamps of the South, the haunts of the prostitute, the Indian lodge, the scientist's laboratory, and the hunter's camp, cataloging the flora, fauna, occupations, and history of the nation. And in all his dazzling images, he speaks in the passionate voice of the individual self.

Like Emerson and Thoreau, Whitman championed the goodness of the self and the creative powers of the imagination. But with a bolder realism that did not flinch at the sordid and painful or retreat to the pastoral, he exposed the hollowness of false selves and urged his readers to break from constricting prejudices. His peculiar democratic vision draws the unshackled individual, freed from the confining slots of gender, race, and class, into a kinship with all Americans and all America.

Whitman's "public road," tramped by a lusty bard and teeming with images from all walks of American life, has snared the fancy of the broadest range of road writers. Less cerebral than Emerson, less censorious than Thoreau, Whitman abandoned system and control for motion and energy. From leisurely picaresque musings to warp-speed careering across the continent, a style of movement auspicious to motor travel, the poet's eye and spirit are restless and insatiable. Excepting only the meditative and elegiac passages, which may be static, and the situated narratives, *Leaves of Grass* is a vision borne by movement, a rush of bold images. Yet as befits the Transcendentalist program, all this movement, all this imaginative exploring of the staggering variety of American lives and landscapes, finally implodes into the self. This self, as Whitman's bard says, "contains multitudes." It revels in a mystical, buoyant unity of all peoples and places.

Most often road writers invoke Whitman casually, as the gypsy poet who inspires or presides over the journey. Beth O'Shea said that her 1922 transcontinental drive with Kit Crandall, recounted in *A Long Way from Boston*, was prompted by her reading of "Walt Whitman . . . and all that company of vagabonds who sang nostalgically of the open road and far horizons" (11). In the late twenties Dallas Lore Sharp told a sceptical academic colleague that he was westward bound for a "baptism of democracy" (41) in Whitman's West, a "beautiful world of new superior [superber] birth" (Sharp 41; Whitman *Leaves* 2:238). In that direction, rather than eastward, where his colleague sought high culture, lay Sharp's Better Country. In 1961 J. R. Humphreys said that "although it was afoot, albeit lighthearted, that Walt Whitman took to the open road, in his *Leaves of Grass* he sounds like one of today's growing band of shun-pikers"— those who travel the backroads in search of folk encounters (29). Such passages contain the germ of more complex and integral applications of Whitman's language and vision in Steinbeck, Heat-Moon, Kerouac, and Saroyan.

The Grapes of Wrath, America's best-known proletarian road saga, furnishes the strongest political test of the redemptive powers of Whitmanesque Transcendentalism in our highway literature. Here the travelers are not vagabonds but refugees; they cannot afford to gild their journey with the tourist's Whitman—so often, as in the foregoing passages, the source of a fanciful posture. Instead, the Transcendental sentiments of Preacher Casy, and by extension Tom Joad, must somehow issue from an essentially naturalistic predicament. Their sentiments cannot be directly attributed to Whitman or Emerson because none of the characters is literate.

When Tom Joad returns to Cherokee County from the McAlister penitentiary he finds that Jim Casy has given up fundamentalist Christianity because he cannot reconcile his lust with his preaching. Casy has begun a different spiritual journey, "thinkin'" his way toward a new vision of humanity—one that does not demean people for their natural behavior. Throughout most of the book he is a thoughtful loner, accompanying the Joads from Oklahoma to California, all the while refusing to invoke "the spirit." His honest skepticism, coupled with bravery and sacrifice, gradually shoulders out pentecostal Christianity as a spiritual force in the lives of the Joads. The novel's evangelicals are increasingly cast as embittered scolds.

By the time he is martyred, Jim Casy has thought his way through to the Emersonian and Whitmanesque vision of "a great big soul" (570), of which each man is a part. There are no longer the just and the unjust, the sheep and the goats, for such moral distinctions, as Whitman said in *Leaves of Grass*, rupture the democratic spirit. In *The Grapes of Wrath* these distinctions spawn division and animosity, as when the addled fundamentalist woman and her cohorts denounce the Weedpatch dance as an orgy. Tom Joad's conversion to Casy's vision, as he relates it to his mother, rolls on in the parallel cadences of Whitman at his messianic best (though more sentimental): "I'll be in the way guys yell when they're mad an'—I'll be in the way kids laugh when they're hungry an' they know supper's ready. An' when our folks eat the stuff they raise an' live in the houses they build—why, I'll be there" (572).

This monologue, which ends John Ford's film version of the novel, fashions a grimly optimistic resolution, in both genres, to the political tensions fomented by the Joads's travails in the fields and on the road. We suffer with them as they abandon the farm, lurch across the Southwest in a jalopy, and scrabble for work in the plantations of California. But as the family disintegrates and an all-or-nothing labor battle looms, Steinbeck suddenly vents the pressure he has so patiently built. He reverts to Whitman's road dream, in which the vagabond poet gathers all experience into a Transcendental unity. The novel's final scene, in which Rose of Sharon suckles a starving man, merely extends the Whitmanesque projection into naturalistic symbolism.

Jim Casy's oversoul includes violence, and he dies for his cause. But it does not provide tactics; it does not tell the Okies or the reader what to do. In this sense Steinbeck fell back on the poetry of the road, succumbing to the lure of abstraction when perhaps he should have pitched a war. As is the case with so many "serious" road books, fiction and nonfiction, movement opens up an imaginative "other space" around the movers, a space that has the potential of defusing or absorbing pain. In *The Grapes of Wrath* the other space, opened up by Jim Casy's folk Transcendentalism, must be projective and abstract, an imaginative extension of physical movement, because the power of the Okies to move through geographical space is inhibited by their poverty.

Casy's secular religion is not fully realized until quite late in the novel, by which time the Joads's misfortunes and sorrows practically defy remedy, spiritual or material. In this respect, while the particular political dilemma of agricultural labor conditions might have been sidestepped, the naturalistic intertia of the book cannot completely be overcome by Casy's oversoul. America's *other* road—that of the cultural alien and the dispossessed—is, rightfully, the novel's popular legacy. Perilous and

84

disorienting, the naturalistic road thwarts Transcendentalist abstraction. Without an economic buffer, its travelers, in order to survive, must view nature in terms of its *use*. From Emerson's perspective in *Nature*, such utilitarian terms are the least conducive to Transcendental enlightenment. In Steinbeck's naturalistic mode, machinery does not spirit refugees through a Romantic landscape that serves as an aid to reflection. In the form of a bulldozer, it destroys their homes. In the form of a tractor, it renders their labor redundant. In the form of a crippled Hudson that becomes the nomadic refuge, it inverts the old agrarian domestic order, replacing the farmer-father with the mechanic-son, the dominant father with the dominant mother. On the road, the "family met at the most important place, near the truck. The house was dead, and the fields were dead; but this truck was the active thing, the living principle. The ancient Hudson, with bent and scarred radiator screen, with grease in dusty globules at the worn edges of every moving part, with hub caps gone and caps of red dust in their places—this was the new hearth, the living center of the family" (135–36).

The naturalistic counterpart to Casy's one big soul is a greasy, rust-bitten machine that supplants organic nature as "the living principle." The road narrative in *The Grapes of Wrath* opens outward not to an imaginatively recreated American wilderness but to the immediate migration of Okies through an unforgiving desert. More often the narrative closes in on the Hudson, so that movement through the wilderness is never divorced from machinery. Steinbeck describes every repair in exhaustive detail, denaturalizing the car in the same way he exposes the toil and hunger that bring fresh peaches to the produce stand. This mechanical precision justifies the anxiety of Al and Tom, whose senses are necessarily absorbed by the Hudson's tics and stutters. Machine consciousness overrides the landscape just as the machine is expected to overcome the land, and all the while we sense, in this naturalistic progression, a bending of human will to physical forces, a surrender that nullifies the most basic Transcendentalist dictum: imagination is more substantial than matter.

Steinbeck segregates his Transcendental and naturalistic messages in *The Grapes of Wrath* to such an extent that they coexist without cancelling one another. Jim Casy is both a visionary and a man of action, but he is not a mechanic. He is attuned to the human spirit, which, like the old Transcendentalists, he cannot reconcile to fundamentalist religion, wage slavery, or complete dependence on machines. Tom Joad is a mechanic as long as his attachment to his family demands that he maintain their Hudson, the new hearth and "living principle." When he turns fugitive, however, he moves out of the sphere of familial duty—away from the Hudson—and into Casy's visionary sphere. The naturalistic story continues despite Tom's conversion, as the flood thwarts virtually every human effort, sweeping away Rose of Sharon's stillborn baby, destroying the crops on which the laborers depend, and immobilizing the Hudson. Rose of Sharon's nursing the stranger signals the perseverance of humankind. But the redemptive symbolism does not finally mitigate or reconfigure the natural and social forces that have driven the starving laborers to such a pass.

The Grapes of Wrath presents conflicting visions of the American road. Whitman's poetic road yields a hopeful yet diffuse vision of democratic unity based on shared travails and dreams. Steinbeck's naturalistic road, realized in the technological and economic particulars of Depression America, evokes quite the opposite spirit: a people divided by class interest, ungovernable economic and natural forces, and sheer bigotry. I see the naturalistic legacy of Steinbeck's novel as the more potent of the two. With the signal exceptions of most African American road narratives and Lars Eighner's *Travels with Lizbeth* (1993), no well-known American highway book before or since *The Grapes of Wrath* has depicted so poignantly the outsider's road, on which the symbolic union of self, landscape, and national myth is fractured.

Blue Highways bears a faint resemblance to *The Grapes of Wrath* in that Heat-Moon employs Whitman as a poetic hedge against unwelcome social and economic developments. Both books describe the displacement of single-family enterprise by corporate organization, and both books mourn the passing of folkways. These very similarities, however, underscore the books' vastly different economic vantages, and hence their quite different Transcendental "solutions" to cultural troubles.

As the creator of Preacher Casy, Steinbeck already "knows" Whitman's Transcendental soul, and he can plot Casy's intellectual struggle out of evangelical strictures and into a vision born of his brutal experience. So although Steinbeck imposes this vision from the top down, so to speak, he creates a character who achieves the vision by testing and rejecting various ideologies from the bottom up. Casy's experience justifies the vision, which spiritually redeems the suffering proletariat. Heat-Moon, on the other hand, plies his Whitman from the outset, from the top down. Whitman's Romanticism glosses his experience and shapes his interpretation of events. Thus the guiding spirit of Whitman is more or less a priori in *Blue Highways*—a vision that is borne out rather than acquired. Moreover, the fictional Casy, while he operates as an observer and a principled sceptic, remains enmeshed in a particular community struggle that continues along the road. Heat-Moon, who says there are "no yesterdays on the road" (168), moves outside the lives and economic battles he encounters, "sampling the peculiarities of place yet cabined off from the sadness of place."

In tandem with Black Elk, the Native American mystic, Whitman serves Heat-Moon as a lyric chorus for his grievances against the bleak future of a consolidated, homogenized America. For example, Whitman's symbol-making may jibe with Heat-Moon's own: "Highway as analog: social engineers draw blueprints to straighten treacherous and inefficient switchbacks of men with curvy notions; taboo engineers lay out federally approved culverts to drain the overflow of passions; mind engineers bulldoze ups and downs to make men levelheaded. Whitman: 'O public road [. . .] you express me better than I can express myself' " (Heat-Moon 39; Whitman, *Leaves* 1:179). Needless to say, Whitman had curvy notions and a superabundance of passion; he also ignored taboos. In "Song of Myself" his vagabond persona says he is the poet of "freedom and extrication" (*Leaves* 1:61). Heat-Moon often takes up this strain of *Leaves of Grass* too, as when he tries to convince a young Portland student to forsake the "consumerist" values of his parents and travel, "undermining routine" (238) as he himself is doing. The gambit fails, and Heat-Moon complains that "student conversations had one theme: Grab!" He says, "The only sensible thing for me, it seemed, was to take my ancient Black Elk and old Whitman and give up on the times" (239). A similar encounter with a melancholy businessman Heat-Moon calls the Boss of the Plains chafes but does not dispel his Whitmanesque faith in the citizenry. This darkly egoistic man "embraced one crisis after another because they gave him significance, something like tragic stature. . . . [he] had found a thousand ways to protect himself from a real confrontation with himself . . . 'Hell under the skull bones,' Whitman calls it" (Heat-Moon 169; Whitman, *Leaves* 1:189).

Presumably a "real confrontation" would yield a brighter, more Transcendental view of life than the Boss could muster. "Unlike other people of the common coin I'd met along the road," Heat-Moon says, "he was separate rather than distinct; yet, unlike his, their commonality sang. They seemed parts of a whole" (172). Here is a fine instance of Heat-Moon's top-down Whitmanesque Transcendentalism. The fact is, he dislikes malcontents of all stripes, as much as he admires eccentric evangels. His stubborn democratic idealism grows wispy and nostalgic when it strikes desperate and angry Americans. Encounters such as these trivialize the Whitmanesque theme of spiritual unity in *Blue Highways* by confusing poetic vision and human nature. As a result, Whitman's idealism becomes nothing more than a personal longing for "harmony" (Heat-Moon's term) which, when it is balked by sad people, accuses them of failure—of something like bankruptcy of spirit.

Heat-Moon invokes Whitman to greater advantage in solitary, contemplative moments, especially when the topic happens to be the old Romantic interplay of self and nature. This epistemological strain, common in Transcendentalist works, features the symbol-making powers of imagination as it fashions versions of the inner self from objects in the world. Though in some instances the automobile may interfere with this process by turning the driver into a passive watcher, most often it serves as an aid to reflection:

> The immensity of sky and desert, their vast absences, reduced me. It was as if I were evaporating, and it was calming and cleansing to be absorbed by that vacancy. Whitman says:
> *O to realize space!*
> *The plenteousness of all, that there are no bounds,*
> *To emerge and be of the sky, of the sun and moon and flying clouds as one*
>   *with them.* (Heat-Moon 196; Whitman, *Leaves* 1:219)

> I looked out the side window. For an instant, I thought the desert looked back. Against the glass a reflection of an opaque face. I couldn't take my attention from that presence that was mostly an absence. Whitman:
> *This the far-on [off] depth and height reflecting my own face,*
> *This the thoughtful merge of myself, and the outlet again.*
> (Heat-Moon 198; Whitman, *Leaves* 1:55)

The freshness of Heat-Moon's diction gives life to the worn notion that Western space paradoxically frees the self as it diminishes the self. But the automobile supplies a new physical dimension to the Transcendentalist scheme. First, it materially propels the observer through space, breaking the "bounds" as only the imagination had done before: it helps the observer "realize space." Second, the car window magically superimposes the driver's face on the Nevada desert so that the Transcendentalist sense of "reflect"—imaginatively finding the self in nature—gains a novel optic spin. In both cases a machine assists the imaginative interplay of self and nature without sundering the Transcendentalist program set forth early on in Emerson's *Nature* and later developed in *Leaves of Grass*.

In similar fashion the movement of the automobile (or bus) through American landscape in *On the Road* imitates the propulsion of Whitman's imagination. Kerouac's lyrical catalogues, often delivered in parallel syntactic repetition, recall Whitman's love of this form and style. In his 1855 preface to *Leaves of Grass* Whitman called the United States "the greatest poem" (2744). Sal Paradise, crossing the Mississippi at St. Louis on his way west, took a page right out of *Leaves*:

> The muddy cobbles and the Montana logs, the broken steamboats, the ancient signs, the grass and ropes by the river. The endless poem. By night Missouri, Kansas fields, Kansas night-cows in the sacred wides, crackerbox towns with a sea for the end of every street; dawn in Abeline. (255)

Even more Whitmanesque (and Eastern, too) is Kerouac's monistic penchant, his longing for the unity of American experience:

> The ferry fires glowed in the night; the same Negroes plied the shovel and sang. . . . as the river poured down from mid-America by starlight I knew, I knew like mad that everything I had ever known and would ever know was One. (147–48)

Of course Kerouac did not give Sal Paradise a Whitmanesque sensibility. *On the Road* is too personal, too desperate; it also lacks Whitman's messianic immunity. But both writers share the urge to evoke an abstract, poetical unity with a profusion of vivid *images*. I emphasize images because in Kerouac, as in Heat-Moon, personal history often jangles the lyric concord of American experience and landscape: it escapes the gravity of poetry and frustrates the Whitmanesque drive.

In fact, Sal Paradise's Romantic epiphanies are Transcendental in manner only. They vent despair and anger with a poetic diction and a cache of geographical images that had become conventional by the mid–twentieth century yet remained a distinct alternative to the language and imagery of commerce and politics. Though Kerouac's language shares Whitman's quirky lyricism, when Sal Paradise utters it, he is straining to convince himself that what he says is true. In place of Whitman's placid exuberance, there is speed chatter, devouring itself and for the moment numbing the sadness of his life.

90

On the Road whistles Whitman in the boneyard of fifties America. A poet of the last century who *celebrated* the goings and comings of his culture with a revolutionary egalitarianism is summoned as a narcotic stay against this century's popular endeavors. Whitman certainly criticized his age—its inhibitions, its class biases, its sexism, its tolerance of slavery: he wanted to loose the mind-forg'd manacles, one and all. But he believed liberation would awaken latent and repressed forces that were basically harmonic and society-loving. Sal Paradise's catalogues, by contrast, are sociopathic exercises in denial and repression—the Dark Romantic speaking the Light Romantic tongue.

Of the modern road writers in whom we hear the words or echoes of Whitman, Saroyan alone does not strain for the poet's effusive animism. When the Whitmanesque voice surfaces in *Short Drive, Sweet Chariot*, it merely intensifies Saroyan's generally buoyant narrative:

> It isn't simply driving at night, it is going on . . . to find out what's out there *now*, not so much along the highway, in the terrain, under the sky, but in the interior of the driver himself. Is he driving out into his sleep, wide awake? Into the sleep of the land? Moving in silence with the sleeping rivers moving, companionate with all sleeping, and all sleepless? Into the sleep with the sleep of the old time, the time of the generations of the animals alone, moving into, and out of their cycles of coming, hunting, having, eating, begating, hiding, and going. (98–99)

Beyond the lyrical parallelisms, which distinguish Whitman's influence from that of other Transcendentalists (and Saroyan names Whitman as an early influence), we again find the automobile drawn into the Romantic interplay of subject and object as a symbol linking interior and exterior journeys. As in Heat-Moon, the car's movement both imitates and provokes the hovering imaginative eye. Thanks to the automobile, which disappears, immediate perception rivals imagination in its power to survey a profusion of images in rapid succession. Thoreau, a lifelong naturalist, complained in *Walden* that the speed of railroad cars blurred the landscape and estranged the traveler from nature: from a moving window one could not see "the country" (47). In *Nature* Emerson introduced the rail passenger's perception as an easy example of philosophical idealism (34). Speed, he said, alters our vantage so rapidly that it jars our perception from its habits and warps ordinary nature into strange forms. This experience serves notice that the mind is not just a neutral recorder of reality, but a shaper of it as well. In these instances both Emerson and Thoreau describe passengers moving toward, by, and beyond a stationary landscape. Saroyan's imaginative movement more nearly resembles Whitman's, freeze-framing images and outstripping even the train's pace across America.

Saroyan's pastoral Romanticism, however, lacks both Whitman's scope of imagery, which often features the ugly and sordid, and the epistemological complexity of Emerson and Thoreau, who labored over the harder issue of how we think as we do, how imagination corrupts or enlightens the mind. He prefers lyric beauty, and sometimes plain sentiment, to both extensions of the Transcendentalist scheme.

In fact, Heat-Moon, though he draws most heavily on Whitman, is the only road writer I have encountered who broaches Emerson's philosophical treatment of idealism in *Nature*. Emerson has reached most modern travel writers through his applied philosophy, found in essays such as "The American Scholar" (1837) and "Self-Reliance" (1841), in which he urged his readers to trust their own impulses and shun the dictates of convention, business, and organized religion.

Only eighty years had elapsed since the publication of "Self-Reliance" when Winifred Dixon, in *Westward Hoboes*, promoted Western auto travel as a means of liberating the self. At Rainbow Bridge in southern Utah she paused to meditate on the connection between authenticity and the desert: "The mere fact of our remoteness helped us shake off layers and layers of other people's personality, which we had falsely regarded as our own and showed us new selves undreamed of. We laugh, at the movies, at the frequency with which the hero goes 'out there, away from all this' to 'find himself.' Yet I think everyone should, once in a while, leave routine and safety behind. . . . Too much security stales the best in us"(274). Emerson argued in "Self-Reliance" that recovering personal independence in solitude was much easier than maintaining that self-trust in society, where pressure to conform is much keener. But the very notion of an authentic self that can be perverted by a socially formed self-consciousness lies at the heart of Emerson's work. Indeed it later became a mainstay of the Transcendentalists' critique of society, and ultimately, as Dixon admitted, an American movie cliche, nonetheless true, she says, for all its triteness. Dixon paired the Transcendental impulse with the now familiar spatial equation: West = the self alone in space = hardy self-reliance and authenticity; East = the self enclosed in capitalist hierarchy = servitude and conformity. The automobile, spatially and hence symbolically, aids in the Transcendental renovation of the self. By doing so, it also overcomes Emerson's objection to the "superstition of Travelling" (277): journeying in the name of self-improvement is pointless if an unchanged self merely changes its place. In Dixon's account the change of place animates the change of self.

In this general point she follows Emily Post's 1915 opinion that the vastness of the plains would sweep the mind clear of pettiness, that "if you could only live with such vastness of outlook before you, perhaps your own puny heart and mind and soul might grow into something bigger, simpler, worthier than is ever likely otherwise" (115). Post's speculation clearly treats the Romantic correpondence between self and nature, and it retains the East-West spatial structure, but it is too diffuse and deterministic to be called Transcendentalist in any strict sense.

Kaj Klitgaard's aesthetics in *Through the American Landscape* verges on Emerson's conception of art in *Nature* as an interplay of landscape and mind producing "an abstract or epitome of the world." "Art," Emerson wrote, is "a nature passed through the alembic of man. . . . The world thus exists to the soul to satisfy the desire of beauty" (19). Klitgaard likewise considered human perception a creative act: "And as for the American landscape being bigger than anybody's picture frame: I consider man's awareness of nature the biggest thing in the universe. Hence art, which serves to sharpen that awareness might be considered the horse pulling the cart into the light"(47). Klitgaard's focus on the artist as the most lively perceiver of nature jibes with Emerson's belief that art is a higher form of beauty than the sort that comes from merely looking at a landscape. More to the point, Klitgaard follows Emerson in placing mind before nature, subject before object. His companion's theory, related in an earlier chapter, that automotive speed engenders new artistic impressions and forms, simply merges Emerson's philosophical idealism with the automobile as a prosthesis of mind.

By far the most outlandish Emersonian gesture in our road literature is found in the rovings of Ken Kesey's Merry Pranksters, whose misadventures are chronicled in Tom Wolfe's *The Electric Kool-Aid Acid Test* (1968). This marriage of Transcendental spirit, psychedelic gambit, road narrative, and New Journalism is all the more remarkable for being a large group undertaking, rare in American road books.[4]

Most sophisticated highway narratives, as we have seen, are symbolic gestures that afford the motorist a special vantage from which to judge society and landscape. Gaining that vantage is the main symbolic act, signifying some theme larger than itself, such as escape, rebellion, discovery, and the like. In most cases road writers have gone out alone or in small company, inconspicuously—as solitary wanderers. The symbolism of their journeys is realized publicly only in the publication of their books. By contrast, the *Acid Test* republicizes a flagrantly public journey in which the travelers brandish their flags. They set out to astonish the bourgeoisie, to lure them out of their "games" and into a radical authenticity.

The staid Emerson would scarcely recognize his philosophy, packaged in the psychedelic colors of the bus FURTHUR and dinning over FURTHUR's woofers and tweeters, but there it is. It is not unadulterated, of course. Hallucinogens add an alien spin, altering perception involuntarily. The Pranksters's addiction to adrenaline is also foreign to Emersonian Transcendentalism, whose spirit lodges in calm reflection. Similarly, the

4. Another example is Douglas Brinkley's *The Majic Bus* (1993), which chronicles a transcontinental bus tour undertaken by his Hofstra University history class.

Pranksters are zealots of candor, often coercing—even humiliating—their fellows into "doing their own thing." This sort of evangelism is anathema to the Emersonian agenda: a fascism of spontaneity.

Wolfe points out that most of the Pranksters (not Cassady) were young people from the middle class who were rebelling against their own class's rules and hierarchies. They balked at the Hell's Angels's anarchic violence, which went too far outside their own upbringing. Thus the FURTHUR juggernaut is largely symbolic and to some extent self-contained. In this way the Pranksters loosely resemble Emerson in that his philosophical rebellion, while radical in its own terms, occurred within the limits of his gentility.

In many other respects the Prankster outlook hews to Transcendentalist ideas, however fervently the trippers claim to be imitating no religion or philosophy. First, the Pranksters, by Wolfe's account, viewed reality and action as allegorical and symbolic, vibrant with meaning. Speed and hallucinogens certainly drove such symbol reading beyond Emerson's desiderata in *Nature* ("Every natural fact is a symbol of some spiritual fact" [20]) into something verging on paranoia, but Wolfe finds the basic Emersonian impulse in Prankster discussions. Second, Wolfe notes the Pranksters' rejection of causality for the direct perception of a cosmic "higher level of reality" (127), an echo of Emerson's rejection of the calculating, materialistic faculty he called the Understanding in favor of Transcendental Reason, which, as Emerson interpreted it, lifts one out of the realm of material cause and effect and into cosmic fusion with the Oversoul. Third, the Pranksters enjoined one another to "do your own thing" without inhibition, to be up-front, emptied of power motives, guile, subtlety, or contrivance. All impressions and feelings were to be expressed ingenuously, innocently, without mediation. As Kesey says, "Everybody is going to be what they are" (65). His essentialism is Emerson's: "What I must do, is all that concerns me, not what the people think" ("Self-Reliance" 263). He argued that "the essence of genius . . . [is] Spontaneity or Instinct" (269), and that "whoso would be a man must be a nonconformist" (261). Finally, the Pranksters reject the

"New York intellectual thing" (100), which involves looking to another country (England or France or India) for a "Fatherland of the mind" (100). Though literary nativism was a strident push by the middle of the nineteenth century, with the Young America movement in Northeastern periodicals, Emerson had delivered his literary declaration of independence to Thoreau's Harvard class of 1837. "The American Scholar" calls for an end to America's bookish hearkening to the "courtly muses of Europe" (70) and a new reliance on indigenous landscape and talent. Nativism in the *Acid Test* is the "American trip:" not the "romantic past" but "tapes, videotapes, tv, movies . . . Buick Electras . . . manic buses, f'r chrissake, soaring, doubledy-clutch doubledy-clutch, to the Westernmost edge" (100–101). Everything good is still on the American highway.

As the trip itself merges with and finally outstrips Transcendentalist philosophy, it is seen as a therapeutic regimen: "They had all voluntarily embarked upon a trip and a state of consciousness that was 'crazy' by ordinary standards. . . . a risk-all balls-out plunge into the unknown, and it was assumed merely that more and more of what was already inside a person would come out and expand, gloriously or otherwise" (78). As a first step, the trip physically removes the individual from domestic and economic entanglements. And as in most travel narratives, such a separation betokens a liberation of personal essence. *The Acid Test*, unlike narratives about solitary wanderers, tells of a divided course of personal "expansion" on the road—that which emerges from the social life inside the bus, and, more conventionally, that which grows out of the landscape and brief social encounters outside the bus.

The bus acts like a "pressure cooker" or an atomic fission chamber: "all traces of freakiness or competition or bitterness or whatever were intensified" (78). Any expansion of consciousness in this context grows out of the sense of sharing the "freak" mission and the response to others' demands for complete frankness and spontaneity. Life on the bus is "like a marathon encounter in group therapy. . . . not for the middle-aged and fucked-up but for the Young and Immune!" (147). The supposed goal is a communal intimacy that supplants both the hierarchy of the nuclear family and government and the cash nexus of capitalism. But Wolfe's narrative, even in its airbrushing of some truly sordid episodes, such as Stark Naked's breakdown in Houston, chronicles a hectic scramble for provisional order—squabbles and bad-trip regimens and power struggles—over which Kesey presides as an avuncular oracle. The feverish anarchy inside the bus tells us quite early on that this communal enterprise, because it is basically solipsistic and stimulus-driven, will quickly starve without the fuel of road novelty.

As in most nonfiction road narratives, fresh landscape and a far-flung citizenry prime the enthusiasm of discovery. But the *Acid Test* breaks new ground in its depiction of the relationship between traveler and territory. In terms of perception the use of hallucinogens is clearly the most radical departure from travel convention, though it was not a new thing in the Pranksters' Romantic heritage. Before the abstemious Transcendentalists, writers like Coleridge and De Quincey were taking bad opium trips and describing fabulous visions as well. In this case, however, the product of drug-spun consciousness is inchoate, merely another example of the Pranksters' quest for intensity and personal transcendence—and the most extreme privileging of subjectivity in our travel literature.

I have tried to show how the automobile shed its essence as a machine as it was absorbed into the rhetoric of Romanticism, and more particularly that of Transcendentalism. The *Acid Test*, while not abandoning this fusion of mind and technology, complicates it by foregrounding technology. The vehicle doesn't disappear; it's shoved in your face. As Prankster historian, Wolfe finds the origins of the FURTHUR ramble in the "fantasy world," the "electro-pastel world" of the suburbs, where the family car is "a huge crazy god-awful-powerful fantasy creature . . . shaped like twenty-seven nights of lubricious luxury brougham seduction—*you're already there, in Fantasyland*, so why not . . . juice it up to what it's already aching to be . . . a whole superhighway long and *soaring, screaming* on toward . . . Edge City, and ultimate fantasies" (35). Here the automobile acts neither as aid to reflection nor as nostalgic time machine. It is an amphetamine. And like the ready cache of diet pills in the medicine cabinet, it serves suburbia in both chore and fantasy—the means of escape built right into the prison. But Wolfe's dithyrambic evocation of automotive ecstasy reminds us that escape from the prison is an end in itself. Fifties technology is its own escape; and yet fifties technology is inescapable. The Pranksters' escape attempt is just an intensified application of suburban tools and toys. But even though this intensity comes at the expense of subjective refinement—an essential part of the old Transcendentalism—the Pranksters self-consciously embraced recreational technology that the stodgy New York intellectuals they visited steadfastly refused. Just as Emerson and Whitman saw the potential for spiritual good in the railroad, despite its anti-pastoral associations, the Pranksters redeemed the automobile, camera, stereo, microphone, and tape recorder from their contemptible reputation among intellectuals.

Such gadgets amplified and duplicated experience, compounding and enriching sensations. Sandy's microphone, for instance, is rigged atop FURTHUR to catch and amplify road sounds, which are broadcast in variable lag to the travelers. Hagen's camera captures "the faces, the faces in Phoenix, the cops, the service-station owners, the stragglers and strugglers of America" (76). You will recall that many road writers have dismissed the cinematic eye as passive and lazy. In the *Acid Test* the movie is a vital metaphor, used by Kesey and taken up by Wolfe, and it has two different meanings, neither connoting passivity. In the non-road sense, the pejorative one, a "movie" is a limited but coherent picture of the world. We might use the term "ideology" the same way: "everybody everywhere, has his own movie going . . . and everybody is acting his own movie out like mad, only most people don't know that is what they're trapped by, their little script." As paraphrased by Wolfe, Kesey explains that the "movie screen of our perceptions . . . closes us out from our own reality" (130). By turning his camera on everbody and everything, Hagen seems to be filming a meta-movie that captures the Pranksters' private movies. Cassady's is *Speed Limit*, Mountain Girl's is *Big Girl*, and so forth. But these personal movies, unlike those of the brutal cops mentioned in the same passage, do not indicate blindness and self-delusion, as

Kesey's observation would suggest. Rather the Pranksters' movies follow the contours of their life experiences.

The road sense of "movie" is closer to Hagen's "great morass of a movie" (131), more inclusive and wide open. It grows out of the camera's inherent power to concentrate and intensify ordinary experience. Like the microphone it makes road reality louder: "a bunch of people roaring across the continental U.S.A. in a bus covered with Day-Glo mandalas aiming movie cameras and microphones at every freaking thing . . . and the U.S. nation streamed across the windshield like one of those goddamned Cinemascope landscape cameras that winds up your optic nerve" (92). The Pranksters' desire for unmediated experience naturally puts a premium on sensation, which is more important than reflection. The travelers who resist the appeal of the cinematic eye do so because it is so alluring it balks reflection: technology threatens to shatter the prosthetic illusion by subduing imagination. Aboard FURTHUR, however, the road movie is *supposed* to outdo imagination. The very fact that it can vindicates the Pranksters' eagerness to embrace electrical gadgetry as yet another way out of the "little script" of the personal movie and into a more intense, if less interpreted, present.

The Pranksters do not think they have much to learn from the people they find along the way, and this lack of curiosity sets their adventure apart from almost every American road account. But the curious blend of contempt and evangelism with which they respond to the citizenry is in some ways more appealing than the patently disingenuous populism oozing from so many road books. Furthermore, the Pranksters' brash defiance of convention on almost every front lays bare the consumption/production duality that is only implicit in other road narratives. Needless to say, the Pranksters produce nothing; their aim is to escape the capitalist movie through costume and play. Day-Glo paint conceals the mass-produced form of the Harvester bus, and whimsical garb (or nudity) distinguishes the travelers from the masses uniformed for service and production. The pleasure of consumption is, as usual, primarily a release from repetition into perpetual novelty. The dependence of one upon the other is repressed, even as the two conditions split into comfortable stereotypes:

> right away this wild-looking thing with the wild- looking people was great for stirring up consternation and vague befuddling resentment among the citizens. The Pranksters were now out among them, and it was exhilarating—look at the mothers staring!... But there would also be people who would look up out of their poor work-a-daddy lives in some town, some old guy, somebody's stenographer, and see the bus and register... delight, or just pure open-invitation wonder. Either way, the Intrepid Travelers figured, there was hope for these people. (61)

Beyond its appeal to whim and its rejection of drudgery, this sensibility, as filtered through Wolfe, veers sharply away from Emerson's Transcendentalism because it takes appearance or behavior as a guide to essence. It is quite possible that looking wild is merely a matter of looking as unlike a stenographer as possible. If so, then one is just the negative of the other. Furthermore, in "The American Scholar" and elsewhere Emerson cautioned his readers against intellectual and linguistic snobbery, urging them to take to the highway, where they could hear coarse and earthy language and appreciate the broad range of American character types. The Pranksters' reverse snobbery—again, as it appears in Wolfe's rendition of the trip—fairly insulates them from this source.

Paradoxically, the FURTHUR experiment provides a rare glimpse into communal travel after Americans had been liberated from rail travel by the automobile early in the century. In doing so it reintroduces inescapable social tension, as opposed to casual encounter, and multiplies responses to the same road experience. The fact that these responses are recorded and edited by an interested third party and not produced by the travelers themselves moves the narrative closer to novelistic treatments of social conflict in a utopian setting, one example of which is Nathaniel Hawthorne's *The Blithedale Romance* (1852). So while the Pranksters may have disdained "the shop, the plow, and the ledger"—precincts that Emerson urged his American scholar to visit (69)—they risked tedium and vexation for a democratic and utopian trial of hipster sensibility.

The legacy of Emerson in the *Acid Test* is thus a mixed one, and it is entangled with Asian religion, Beat manners, and Kesey's personal take on enlightenment. Wolfe's frenetic impressionism, designed to imitate the lingo and nerve of the Pranksters, often beggars its subject. And especially when his style feels like a crazy mask for banality, it seems that the Transcendentalist strain in *Acid Test* owes more to Wolfe than to the Pranksters. In any event, his chronicle, one of the few boldly original American road books, not only testifies to the perseverance and protean adaptabilty of Emerson's ideas, it serves as a foil for road books taking their cue from Henry David Thoreau's solitary and at times misanthropic brand of New England Transcendentalism.

Near the end of his journey William Least Heat-Moon was needled by a reclusive historian who, paraphrasing *Walden*, pointed out that "Thoreau traveled extensively in Concord" (389; *Walden* 4). The historian implied that perhaps Heat-Moon had not learned Thoreau's lesson: "the swiftest traveller is he that goes afoot" (*Walden* 47). The recluse's gibe reminds us that there is a contradiction in Thoreau's tremendous popularity with American road writers. He was a naturalist who crafted a revered critique of American society in the middle nineteenth century out of things he found in his own hometown. He worked from the local outward, the "deepest" kind of travel.

The only road writer I encountered who addressed this paradox directly was Dallas Lore Sharp, who wrote in *The Better Country* (1928) that

We ought to travel by foot, of course, if we would rightly travel. . . . But who sings the praises of walking nowadays? Or who could in this land, which, from the Foundation, was intended for motor cars and airplanes? Nothing in the Arabian Nights sounds stranger in these footless times and on our motored highways than an essay like

Thoreau's on walking. It could hardly have been written now for
very lack of walking words. . . . the language of locomotion now . . .
reduc[es] our whole sublime continent to the figment of miles. (46)

The whole settled continent beggars Thoreau's method, Sharp argued,
and thus demands, and fosters, a fresh parlance, yet one still capable of
conveying Thoreau's ideas. As we have seen, Sharp changed the baseline
for intimacy with landscape and people, contending that driving, in
contrast with rail travel, is "an intimate, immediate mode of travel"
that brings one "close to the earth and the people" (31). He thus deftly
exempted the automobile from Thoreau's warning that mechanical speed
is always purchased at the cost of excess labor and alienation from the
land. In most road books that allude to Thoreau or invoke his ideas,
the automobile simply spirits travelers away from routine and habit
and confinement (Concord), and into the open spaces, where reflective
criticism is nurtured (Walden Pond). In Thoreau's terms, he symbolically
forsakes the scene of production for the scene of contemplation. In road
narratives, as we have seen, contemplation must be bound up with both
production and consumption, and as such it cannot take place outside
the capitalist process that makes it possible. At some level it must endorse
the thing it ostensibly opposes.

Sharp understands that compared with the Native Americans he
encounters he is the product of "an alien, mechanistic, materialistic education" (188). He understands as well that he lives in a "mechanical age"
in which people are the "victims of [their] own machines" (95), the "tools
of their tools," as Thoreau put it (33). And yet despite Sharp's admission
that the automobile is a "Mechanical Monster" bred out of the need to
cross vast distances (45), his Romantic trajectory is shaped by this central
tool of his century, which is from the outset of his trip naturalized—even
at times a Transcendental symbol akin to Thoreau's sunsets or loons.

When Sharp, a retired college teacher, leaves the Northeast with his
wife and begins his search for "the Better Country," he follows convention
by couching his design in literary and symbolic terms:

I was answering some racial urge, following the migratory line and the restless hope of my people. "Every sunset which I witness," says Thoreau, "inspires me with the desire to go to a West as distant and as fair as that into which the sun goes down. He appears to migrate westward daily, and tempt us to follow him". . . . Thoreau did not go far West. One does not need to if one goes on foot . . . "My needle . . . always settles between west and south-southwest. The future lies that way to me, and the earth seems more unexhausted and richer on that side." (41)

The passages Sharp quotes are from "Walking" (609, 607). In this essay Thoreau designs and elaborates a symbolic opposition between eastward and westward movement. "I must walk toward Oregon," he says, "and not toward Europe. And that way the nation is moving, and I may say that mankind progress from east to west" (608). "It is hard," he continues, "for me to believe that I shall find fair landscapes or sufficient wildness and freedom beyond the eastern horizon. . . . Let me live where I will, on this side is the city, on that the wilderness" (607).

Thoreau also employs this polarity when he contrasts walking on forest paths and walking on highways. He shuns roads, which "are made for horses and men of business" (604). They connect towns for purposes of commerce, and the people who stay on them "are wayworn by the travel that goes by and over them, without traveling themselves" (604). "If you would go to the political world, follow the great road,—follow that market-man, keep his dust in your eyes, and it will lead you straight to it." Thoreau chooses to "pass from it as from a bean-field into the forest, and it is forgotten" (603). Those who do not walk at all are associated with the eastern space, reserved for tradition and production. "I am astonished by the power of endurance, to say nothing of the moral insensibility, of my neighbors who confine themselves to shops and offices for . . . years almost together" (600). In short, "Eastward I go only by force; but westward I go free" (607).

How easily Thoreau's binary rhetoric is taken up by the motorist, who follows the market-man and says he is going into the forest! Once the goals of walking become the goals of driving, and it is driving that now frees us from the world of politics and commerce into the western wilderness, the way is paved for the automobile to serve any number of Transcendentalist purposes.

To begin with the most extreme instance, I return to Sharp's prairie afflatus, the quasi-mystical moment on the high plains of Kansas when he says that "the wheels of my being synchronized perfectly with the wheels of my going, all that was within me meshing with all that was without, my spirit sliding from first to second, from second into high and back into reverse without grabbing of the clutch or any clashing of the gears" (110–11). Strictly speaking, Sharp borrows from Emerson here, and not Thoreau, specifically the "transparent eye-ball" passage from *Nature*, in which Emerson, walking in the forest, feels "uplifted into space. . . . I become a transparent eye-ball; I am nothing; I see all; the currents of the Universal Being circulate through me" (10). The old Transcendentalist afflatus, intuitive and ecstatic, remains fairly intact in content, and it occurs when it should, as the subject reflects upon itself and nature in a pastoral setting (the West, where one goes free). Only the metaphor changes—but what a change. In Emerson the unifying spirit behaves like air or water, a circulating current. In Sharp, it's a gearbox. The automobile has become a machine that completely sheds the usual connotations of "machinery"—coldness, mindlessness, mass production, unnaturalness, utility, commerce—and joins, indeed displaces, the nature symbol as a conduit of spirit. It ferries Sharp to the Southwest Native American reservations, where he longs to be an Indian and forget his "mechanistic" and "materialistic" education (186, 188), yet another point of sympathy with Thoreau, who read widely about Native American cultures and praised their material austerity in *Walden*.

Just as Thoreau shuns the narrow road to the "political world" in "Walking," he makes much of abandoning all routine at Walden Pond: "My days were not days of the week, bearing the stamp of any heathen deity, nor were they minced into hours and fretted by the ticking of a clock; for I lived like the Puri Indians, of whom it is said that 'for yesterday, today, and tomorrow they have one word'" (102). Sharp follows suit during his own automotive retreat: "I would break training now. If there was a moral order in the universe, I would keep hands off. The Best Minds at Washington, the buying and selling of seats in the Senate, Teapot Dome . . . all of this I would forget. . . . nor consult another time-table, nor own another alarm clock, nor care what day of the week it is, what hour of the day" (113). In a lengthy encomium on the vanity of fashion in *Walden*, Thoreau compares our clothes with skins and shells shed by animals and insects: "Our outside and often thin and fanciful clothes are our epidermis, or false skin, which partakes not of our life, and may be stripped off here and there without fatal injury" (21). Likewise Sharp eschews boiled shirts: "I had split and shed that false front in the tonneau as a cicada sheds its skin" (113).

Zephine Humphrey, in *Green Mountains to Sierras*, takes up Sharp's Thoreauvian refrain—most audibly, again, in the desert Southwest. Like Sharp and Thoreau before him, she finds in Native American cultures a stark alternative to Western materialism and environmental exploitation. And like Sharp, she borrows Thoreau's philosophy to explain the contrast:

> I felt as if my native, far-flung America, had all my life been fashioning me in ways which I little suspected; and, through the chemistry of her soil, the [a]fflatus of her winds and streams, the persuasion of her seasons, had developed in me a kinship with her elder children, the only truly native Americans. . . . Intensely I understood the simplicity and serenity of their lives. Here [Taos] was a people which had always known and had never abandoned the economy of adjustment which our burdened, extravagant, unhappy generation is striving so feverishly to discover. (76)

This is an adequate summary of the "Economy" section of *Walden*, in which Thoreau condemns his century's getting and spending and demonstrates how to achieve some semblance of the "simplicity and nakedness of man's life in primitive ages" (33) by assuming the vantage of a "voluntary poverty" from which to recognize conventional "luxuries" as the "positive hindrances" they really are. He repeatedly turns to "the customs of some savage nations" that might "be profitably imitated by us," such as the busk of the Mucclasse Indians, the purifying ritual of burning all possessions once a year (61).

Perhaps it goes without saying, but bourgeois motorists like Sharp and Humphrey are fond of Thoreau's austerity because it has devolved into a stance. It has an intellectual cachet and the vague appeal of hearty individualism, self-sacrifice, and gentle rebellion. But as a romanticized stance—a packaged intellectual commodity—it no longer requires real sacrifice, as Robert Pirsig notes in *Zen*. Much like the historical pastoral, Thoreau's asceticism provides a politically attractive and attractively disposable riff for the motorist who can equate driving out West with walking at Walden. At its most brittle, it sounds ridiculous: "I remember once reading what some old wise chap said about simplicity—keeping clear of fashion and meanness and hurry, you know, in order to have an unobstructed vision for greatness!" says the Wilbys' Mrs. Eastcott as she cruises the West in the 1912 novel *On the Trail to Sunset* (146). Her Anglophilic diction and boosterism are both so strikingly out of kilter with Thoreau they reveal how handily the subversive is absorbed by the conventional. In more abstract terms, the whole capitalist enterprise underpinning automobile travel simply reproduces itself by incorporating its antithesis: the driver claims that driving west is tantamount to moving outside the whole cycle of production and consumption, whereas the experience of driving west is so fetchingly described it becomes one of the most compelling reasons to continue the practices Thoreau detested.

The only road writer who has managed to avoid this contradiction did not drive at all. Lars Eighner hitchhiked. His chronicle of the three years he spent on the road and on the streets with his dog, *Travels with Lizbeth*, is a sort of urban *Walden* in which dumpster diving, "a modern form of self-reliance" (124), stands in stead of Thoreau's recycling of lumber and nails for his cabin. Though neither hermit nor ascetic, Eighner makes a virtue of his resourcefulness, focusing, like Thoreau, on the basics of survival while moralizing on the excesses of the culture he has provisionally abandoned: "I was shocked to realize that some things are not worth acquiring, but now I think it is so. Some material things are white elephants that eat up the possessor's substance" (124). Eighner's narrative departs from those of his fellow Thoreauvians in his lack of power to consume, and hence his ability to insulate his travels. Because he is poor, he is at the mercy of hunger, thieves, and the police in ways that even Thoreau never was. His deep-travel story demonstrates that in the late twentieth century, in a settled nation, stepping outside the capitalist system exacts a greater toll than it did in old Concord. Thoreau was a curiosity; Eighner is an outlaw.

The voice of the true outsider in American road books, Transcendentalist or no, never settles into the dabbler's equanimity. African American voices are bitter or combative or sad or frightened. Henry Miller's is hot and preachy. Eighner's is staid, anachronistic and condescending.

And Robert Pirsig's is vengeful and arrogant. Though *Walden* is the book he packs in his cycle's saddlebags (it "can be read a hundred times without exhaustion" [36]), its spiritual residue in *Zen* must be found in Pirsig's Buddhism, his studied austerity, his misanthropy, and his Jeremiads on American culture.[5] Pirsig, unlike Thoreau, conceives his message in personal terms, so that his social criticism seems the issue of a grudge. Like Sigal before him, Pirsig does not suffer fools (read everyone but himself) gladly. His humorless diatribes, again foreign to Thoreau's sensibility, often verge on the grandiose, if not the messianic.

Still, for all its vexing self-importance, *Zen* remains the only autobiographical road narrative to challenge the epistemological prejudices that underwrite so many other road books. Specifically, he seeks to correct the modern split between subject and object that has estranged us from technology, rendering the machine (in this case a motorcycle) an embodiment of larger industrial forces generally thought to be sinister and

5. Sacvan Bercovitch treats the tradition of the American Jeremiah in *The American Jeremiad* (1978).

inscrutable. In a broader sense Pirsig returns to the Transcendentalists' attempts to repair the subject-object split in the nineteenth century, with the difference that Pirsig involves technology more deeply on the object side of the dichotomy in place of the Transcendentalists' pastoral nature.

Considering Dallas Lore Sharp's Kansas epiphany and the larger naturalizing of the automobile it represents, it may be objected that there is no such rift and thus no need to patch it. Pirsig rightly observes, however, that the machine can be greened only when it works. When it fails, it becomes an impediment, if not an antagonist, and its connection to the faceless walls of Eastern industry is felt anew. Thus he distinguishes between the "Romantic" and "Classic" modes of knowledge, neither of which is in itself, according to Pirsig, complete. His Romantic traveler lives on the "cutting edge of experience" (254), a subject registering a series of impressions but taking his machine for granted *when it works*. This attitude applies to most of our travel writers. The Classic mode of knowledge views the automobile or motorcycle only as a mechanism, completely disjunct from the traveler's perceptions. When the Romantic traveler is forced to confront his conveyance as a machine, the old harmony is sundered; likewise, the mechanic, and the industrial worker who makes the machine, cannot work backward into the subject and discover the organic nature of the machine.

According to Pirsig, this division of Romantic subject and Classically engineered object has been responsible for the modern antipathy between technology and self-fulfillment—an opposition realized so often in American road books in the symbolic difference between East and West, repetition and novelty, conformity and impulse, factory and desert. He proposes to mend this split in two ways. The first is mystical and Eastern:

> I think that [my friends'] flight from and hatred of technology is self-defeating. The Buddha, the Godhead, resides quite as comfortably in the circuits of a digital computer or the gears of a cycle transmission as he does at the top of a mountain or in the petals of a flower. (16)

The second is epistemological and Western. It depends upon what the Sophists called *arete* and Pirsig calls "Quality"—an understanding of the world not in terms of mastery or transcendence, but in terms of harmony with matter:

> And now Phaedrus [Pirsig's lost alter-ego] began to see for the first time the unbelievable magnitude of what man, when he gained powers to understand and rule the world in terms of dialectical truths, had lost. He had built empires of scientific capability to manipulate the phenomena of nature into enormous manifestations of his own dreams of power and wealth—but for this he had exchanged an empire of understanding of equal magnitude: an understanding of what it is to be a part of the world, and not an enemy of it. (342)

In practical terms, Quality would usher us "back into the craftsmanlike self-involved reality" in which "there is no subject and there is no object" (253, 261). Presumably he has in mind a revival of the late nineteenth-century protests of artisans against the intrusion of capitalism in the arena of production (Lasch 215). But the political realization of Quality is clearly Transcendental in any case, arising from self-improvement and not from an organized political effort. "The place to improve the world is first in one's own heart and head and hands, and then to work outward from there," Pirsig argues (267), following the principle of Thoreau in "Resistance to Civil Government" (1849) and Emerson in "Politics" (1844) that real political change cannot be won by external force, which is always expedient rather than essential, but by individual cultivation, which will ultimately change the character of the group. This principle fuels Pirsig's thoroughgoing distrust of all thought produced by institutions as nothing more than the interested reproduction of the institutions themselves (cf. 354), a complaint registered often by Emerson, most pointedly in his attack on organized religion in "The Divinity School Address" (1838).

In his pursuit of Quality, Pirsig goes the Transcendentalists one better in his conclusion that "no books can guide us anymore" (202). In

"The American Scholar" Emerson relegates books to the thinker's "idle times," scolding the "bookworm" for merely repeating "accepted dogma" instead of thinking for himself (58). But Emerson acknowledges, like Thoreau, that the classics might inspire an original thinker. Curiously, Pirsig's own declaration of intellectual independence, which occurs more than halfway through *Zen*, grows particularly out of his dissatisfaction with *Walden*: "The book seems tame and cloistered, something I'd never have thought of Thoreau, but there it is. He's talking to another situation, another time, just discovering the evils of technology rather than discovering the solution. He isn't talking to us" (202). In other words, Thoreau perceives the estrangement of people from technology in a scarcely industrialized earlier America, but cannot anticipate the pervasive involvement of machinery in modern life, which cannot be comprehended in a simple duality. Pirsig wants to push beyond this duality so that both the creator and the user of technology will feel a Zen-like "identity" with the machine (261). Such harmony would, in the realm of sensibility, break down the Romantic/Neoclassic dualism of perception, and, in the realm of economics, return production to the hands of artisans. The first change, by bringing consumption nearer production, would lessen the suspicion and ignorance of "Romantic" consumers who, by turning their backs on technology, effectively make it easier for producers to manipulate consumers. Consumers no longer at odds with technology could therefore, one by one and in due time, work harmoniously with producers to create more durable and environmentally friendly machines.

Pirsig's meditations, though they arise from a very conventional backroads escape from commerce and institutions, expose the usual self-cancelling logic of such gestures. Travelers who flee the sites of production for a wilderness space in which to recreate the self are trying to maintain an impossible and harmful mental dualism by escaping its material trappings. This flight blinds the traveler to that part of the self which is inextricably bound to technology; in so doing, it assures a complacency that will allow capitalist industry to further control the means and ends of production.

It is only in the arena of modern technology that Pirsig in the end strays from his Transcendentalist mentors, for his philosophical goal is from the beginning to repair the old subject-object dualism—a problem that was, in America, troubling Jonathan Edwards as early as the eighteenth century, but one that did not find its earliest full treatment here until the Transcendentalists took it up with sanguine purpose. Pirsig's originality lies in his point that the Transcendentalist "object" has grown much more complex and stubborn with the industrialization of America.

From Whitman's lyric egalitarianism to Emerson's mystic individualism to Thoreau's ascetic economy, the Transcendentalists have left American road writers a cache of models and responses with which to frame their journeys. The most pervasive legacy compels travelers to treat their wanderings as symbolic gestures, setting themselves outside the mainstream for the purposes of reflection upon self and society. The trip may symbolize rebellion against convention, a baptism in nature, a recovery of self-determination, mystical self-fulfillment, liberation from routine, a search for lost simplicity, or, as in the case of the Joads, a discovery of democratic unity. With few exceptions, the trip holds out the promise of realizing the opposite of American mass culture in the twentieth century, of breaking its industrial gravity and forming a new center in the nonconforming individual or group.

But as Pirsig has made plain, Transcendental fantasies are often conjured out of a failed dualism, resulting in a history of road narratives that recapitulate the gesture of rebellion without examining its terms. African American road books from the fifties onward shatter this neo-Transcendentalist illusion of the outer vantage because the travelers in these narratives simply cannot get there.

The Nigger Window: Black Highways
and the Impossibility of Nostalgia

4

Though Ralph Ellison's *Invisible Man* was generally acclaimed when it appeared in 1952, Irving Howe complained in *The Nation* that Ellison had embraced an escapist Emersonian solution to the problem of Negro identity in America (454). Through hard experience, the novel's protagonist comes to understand that as long as he looks to others, of any race, as the source of his identity, he can do nothing but reflect the traits of a very limited number of black stereotypes, from Uncle Tom intellectual to leftist radical to sexual athlete. Only when he understands that he is in fact invisible, a blank space occupied by a succession of ideological holograms, does he feebly discern the Transcendentalist remedy—faith in an intrinsic nature unique to himself. But *Invisible Man* has more to do with the disease than the inoculation. Its Transcendental content, though Promethean, remains a smoldering, obscure impulse damped by enormous social restrictions.

Emerson's ideal self—the cocky, unselfconscious adolescent of "Self-Reliance"—is meant to remind men cowed and burdened by the social expectations they have internalized that once in their lives they were free and to encourage them to recover that freedom by banishing the gaze of the "other" from their awareness. The internalized "other," however, is one thing for a middle-class white person of Emerson's time or our own and quite another for an African American. Emerson and Thoreau were aware of the psychic tyranny of conventional roles and images, not to mention the strain of class and labor, but the vestiges of their Romantic versions of self-reliance presuppose a subject who already enjoys a material and cultural independence by virtue of his or her race. So the business of silencing the internalized "other" requires for a beginning some basic economic independence, and white skin has in America always been a currency in itself. While the Transcendentalists' recuperative program may offer a psychic defense for anyone, including black Americans, trapped in the projections of the "other," it has more commonly been invoked in Anglo highway books as a therapeutic pastime with a literary cachet, or perhaps a subjective theme, something to elevate the contemplative side of travel to a higher, "literary" plane.

At least since long-distance car travel became practicable—since Dreiser metaphorically allied rail travel with mass production and automobile travel with individual consumption—nonfiction highway narratives have generally linked spatial, economic, and personal independence. Moving away from industrial and mercantile centers of production (or in any case the workplace) has signalled the freedom to spend without producing, to see without being watched—by bosses or train passengers. The static and repetitive is replaced by the kinetic and random. Alienated labor is replaced by the "work" of consuming, which is really the power to make others work for you. As we have seen, Transcendentalist messages about self-determination, contemplation, immersion in nature, and the rejection of routine and superfluous labor are easily absorbed into the rhetoric of subject-centered highway narratives. However, these messages not only conceal the reversal of economic roles involved in most highway journeys—from worker to consumer—they presuppose the privilege to consume, with enough privacy to allow pleasurable contemplation in the bargain.

African American nonfiction road narratives invert the economy that subsidizes mainstream Transcendental or contemplative themes. In these accounts the self is not freed into neutral self-examination by anonymity, the absence of bosses, and the power to consume. Instead, the driver becomes a product offered for the scrutiny of other consumers. Self-consciousness, in this reversal, still hinges on the gaze of the consumer, but the consumer is the vendor. John A. Williams, on assignment with *Holiday* magazine, had just begun his 1963 cross-country drive when he was denied service at a New England lunchroom. Thereafter, he found himself "picking out places to stop or, rather, letting them pick me out. It worked like this: you begin to drive more slowly. The eye drifts over this motel or that, seeking some instinctive assurance that you will not have to put your life on the line by asking for a single for the night" (26). Near Lemhi Pass in Idaho, where Meriwether Lewis first crossed the Divide and where many Anglo motorists later confessed to a *frisson* in their passages, Williams was denied a motel room. The clerk had asked her husband, who was watching *Gunsmoke*, "Do you want him or don't you?" (99). In New Orleans Williams mistakenly walked into a white restaurant. "The bartender came running toward me. 'Outside. I'll take your order from the window.' He pointed to the rectangular window. So that, I thought with some vague amusement, was the Nigger Window" (67).

Not far from where Williams would be directed to the Nigger Window four years later, John Howard Griffin stained his skin and undertook "to discover if America was involved in the practice of racism against black Americans" (161)—a purpose that sounds impossibly naive only because it is hard to recover the skepticism at which it was aimed. Before he began his bus-and-hitchhiking journey to Atlanta, Griffin, already darkened, once caught himself examining the posted menu outside Brennan's in New Orleans:

> I read the menu carefully, forgetting that Negroes do not do such things. It is too poignant, like the little boy peering in the candy store window. It might affect the tourist.
>
> I looked up to see the frowns of disapproval that can speak so plainly and so loudly without words. (45)

"It might affect the tourist." In this case the power of consuming extends to the power of denying its opposite; if Griffin is seen reading the menu, he becomes a part of Brennan's—a part of the menu, a part of the building, a part, even, of the Vieux Carre—and he represents not a gracious servant (he *could* be a "kitchen boy" [45]), which would be consonant with the restaurant's image, but a pathetic, and hence subversive, outcast. The very desire to purchase, demonstrated in such a way, violates the unspoken contract of racial separation by calling attention to it and by arousing improper sympathies for its victims.

When he rode a bus into Mississippi, Griffin was denied a bathroom at rest stops, but when he hitchhiked, he lost even the shred of privilege afforded by a bus ticket. By day he could not peddle himself. After dark, however, he suddenly found himself a commodity prized by white men who picked him up "as they would pick up a pornographic photograph or book." All of these men "showed morbid curiosity about the sexual life of the Negro as an inexhaustible sex-machine with oversized genitals and a vast store of experiences . . . things they themselves ha[d] never dared to do" (85). In one instance a scholarly young man who had couched his sexual curiosity in the terms of academic inquiry ultimately asked Griffin to expose himself, a request Griffin politely declined (88).

At the heart of these encounters Griffin sensed a specious bonhomie on the part of his rides. They assumed that under cover of darkness, in the privacy of a car, they could establish common emotional ground through manly intimacy or frank discussion. Perhaps they had fooled themselves, believing, like Kerouac's Sal Paradise, that Griffin was one of the enviable "happy, true-hearted, ecstatic Negroes of America" (180), unencumbered by the rules of white society, and that under cover of darkness, in the privacy of a car, they could innocently and good-naturedly join in the fun. In any case, Griffin found that the automobile provided a dangerous mix of seclusion, privilege, and confinement. It was a place where, as Ralph Ellison's young Invisible Man also discovered when he chauffeured a similarly curious white philanthropist, public inhibitions vanished. The intimacy of the cab, depicted so often in road literature as a condition in which strangers can speak candidly to one another, obtains in Griffin's narrative as well, except that the black passenger is its hostage, powerless to reject its terms. The white ride, on the other hand, is free to confuse coercion with get-down frankness.

As Carl Rowan began the first leg of his trip across the South by car, train, and bus in 1951, preparing to write *South of Freedom*, his first concern lay with the risks of service on the road. As an outsider and a black man he knew he was endangered by his ignorance of the history of every town and its vendors, an ignorance that exposed him to violent men who lynched negroes for "dressing and acting like white folks" (17): "As I drove that rented car through cracker-barrel hamlets . . . I realized that I had come face to face with doubt. Doubt as to which filling station would allow me to buy gasoline and also to use the toilet. Doubt as to which restaurant would sell me food, even to take out. . . . I would be prepared to answer if addressed as 'boy,' to smile if a white man insulted me under circumstances where he obviously was in power" (16, 18).

If the legal conditions with regard to race had changed radically almost thirty years later, when Chet Fuller, a black reporter from Atlanta, went on the road as both a reporter and a poor laborer to see how racial feelings had changed since the publication of Griffin's *Black Like Me*, the African American traveler in the South enjoyed little more ease. Fuller discovered that when he forfeited the protection of a business suit, the newspaper office, and a home in the suburbs, "gas-station attendants, cashiers in grocery stores and cafeterias, people all over seemed to look at me differently, as if they were not really seeing me" (7). When his car broke down at night on an isolated stretch of I-85 in North Carolina he recalled the story of a black man who only two years before had been castrated and dumped in a river. At a service station he found "the toughest bunch of rednecks this side of Billy Carter's service station in Plains. When I stuck my head in the door, all conversation and laughter halted immediately. There was total silence for at least ten seconds. They all looked at me in amazement, then looked at one another. I knew they were all saying to themselves: 'Well goddamn. Am I seeing things or did a nigger just stick his head in here?' The ache in my balls got more severe. I wanted to turn and run" (27). Riding with the driver dispatched to tow his car, Fuller says that he "didn't trust him as far as I could throw his scrawny carcass after busting his skull with the heel of my hand—which is what I planned to do to defend myself, if anything went awry. . . . in the back of my mind, I kept wondering what the hell I was doing here in the first place, in the dark, in the cab of a truck on the highway, probably about to get castrated or worse" (29).

As it turns out, the driver is friendly and encourages Fuller to settle in North Carolina, which he declares to be a more racially tolerant state than Alabama or Georgia. The tough rednecks fix his car cheaply and quickly, and they make a point of their fairness. Fuller wonders at his alarm, but though in this instance he regrets it, he does not disown it. In the course of this Gothic episode, which occurs early in *I Hear Them Calling My Name*, Fuller reveals that his misguided rage feeds on a number of imaginative associations. He recalls the castrated man from a news story printed in his paper, *The Atlanta Journal*. Some of his black friends have urged him to carry a gun because "you stop at some of these filling stations without your stuff [gun], in some of these small towns, these crackers liable to do anything" (34). And he recollects "all the legends" of racial violence in the South (34).

But Fuller brings to his travels a set of images his predecessors had not known: menacing crackers from television, "Burt Reynolds redneck movies," and *Deliverance* (27, 33). These types, broadened and main-streamed by Hollywood for comic or Gothic ends, had by the late seventies become staples of armchair regionalism, and Fuller, who had not lived in the rural South, understandably mingled them with other threatening historical, anecdotal, literary, and personal associations. If anything, the image of the screen cracker had eclipsed (and in some cases outlived) other perceived threats in the South, even for white travelers.

The objective distinction between what is real and what is imaginary for the black traveler does nothing to dispel the fear and suspicion that have denied that traveler the Romantic possibilities of suspension from work or history. Fuller says that despite even the historical progress made in "the civil rights movement, the black movement, voting rights; after all the things that were supposed to help remove the veil of ignorance and darkness from the South—I still did not feel safe traveling alone in my native region. And no other black person I knew felt any safer" (35).

Only the traveler's attitude has changed in Eddy Harris's 1993 *South of Haunted Dreams*. Harris motorcycles South as a "racist" (31) and a "road warrior" (51), fairly spoiling for a fight. Just before leaving he is detained by the police for walking into an upscale St. Louis shopping district. And he gets no farther than Bowling Green, Kentucky, before he is shown a seat alone in the back of a cafe, where he is left to wonder if someone has spit in his food. But though his journey is haunted by such suspicions, in the end he has encountered mostly friendly service.

As long as the history of persecution broods over an African American journey, the characteristic postures of American highway travel are impossible. The traveler's relations to historical landmarks, the landscape, regional peculiarities (including services), contemplative solitude, and space itself are formed and guided by the traveler's sense of control—intellectual, economic, racial, and sometimes sexual control. Typically, in Anglo American road books the myth of conquest is reborn, either nostalgically or ironically or both, in an expansive desire for novelty, anonymity, discovery, and intellectual mastery, a desire tacitly underwritten by the privilege of race. In these books history appears as a sequence of events to be condemned or nostalgically savored by a traveler who stands (rhetorically, at least) outside them.

All the black travelers mentioned in this chapter seek intellectual mastery as well, in the sense that they travel to generalize and interpret, and all view history as a sequence of events. The difference is that (Griffin excepted) they cannot yet enjoy a vantage outside the forces and events they observe. Indeed their keen awareness of an historically manufactured identity throws into relief both the Transcendental posture, with its defiance of convention and its optimistic egoism, found in writers like Sharp, Duncan, and (sometimes) Heat-Moon, and the darker Romantic posture, with its turbulent, manic-depressive egocentricity, found in writers like Sigal and Kerouac. Black travelers have simply been bound by history in ways that white travelers have not. Their subjectivity has been dominated by awareness and fear of the white observer who wields both psychological and material power. Unlike the boss or family or routine the white traveler abandons to discover America or himself, the black traveler cannot shed his blackness, for it is a condition impervious to distance. He can't say, with Peter S. Beagle, that out West "you could be anything you wanted to be in this land" (107). It was driving not in the South but on the northern Great Plains that John Williams found himself constantly stared at as he drove. On one lonely stretch a man eagerly pointing Williams out to his family lost control of his car and spun off the road (96). It is no wonder that in place of the elaborate outfitting described in many Anglo narratives *This Is My Country Too* opens with "psychological preparation," including the question of whether he should travel armed (he did not).

In African American road narratives the naturalistic mode is more pronounced than Romantic, Transcendental, or pastoral modes. Romantic topics such as self-discovery and imaginative projection, for example, arise naturally enough in any nineteenth- or twentieth-century autobiographical account, and black road narratives are no exception. These topics are given their naturalistic spin by an emphasis on social and economic forces that thwart desire in any form—repose, pastoral joy, the freedom to consume, historical nostalgia, nostalgia for the present, or a yearning for friendship with strangers. In a sense, Rowan, Griffin, Williams, Fuller, and (to a degree) Harris revisit, much later, the hard country traveled by fictional white characters in Hamlin Garland's *Main-Travelled Roads* (1891), Upton Sinclair's *The Jungle* (1906), Steinbeck's *The Grapes of Wrath*, and Dos Passos's *The 42nd Parallel*. In these books, of course, highway perils are economic rather than racial, but the road likewise denies the traveler, who is usually a refugee, any sort of escape or freedom. It signifies instead despair and helplessness, a continuation of historical circumstances rather than a reprieve. The traveler remains an alien—not the Romantic alien of the Beats or their ersatz brethren, not even the semi-ironic picaro like Nelson Algren's Dove Linkhorn, but someone shunned and vulnerable, unable to penetrate the local, always on guard. White writers may pick up alienation as a theme, as a feature of their projected discontent or their dissatisfaction with American culture, but they may also lay it down again.

Likewise, although Anglo travelers have, from the beginning of highway narratives until now, complained of unfriendly treatment at the hands of slackwater cops, compared with the humiliations black travelers have suffered from the police such encounters feel, by contrast, like narrative contrivances designed to trouble the surface of an ordinary trip. Peter Beagle understood the difference well. In 1964 he and his motorcycling companion Phil Sigunick were arrested in Salina, Kansas, on suspicion of vagrancy but allowed to go when they produced traveler's checks. "Lucky we weren't black. . . . If we'd been black . . . Jesus" (70). Just the year before, John Williams had been stopped in Illinois, California, Kentucky, and Ohio and followed in Georgia, Tennessee, and Mississippi: "Followed, pulled over, and made to know that I was a lone black man in a big car, and vulnerable as hell" (131). In the South Williams traveled only at night, "hiding from the police in small towns" (81). In 1951 Rowan steeled himself to "dance a little jig," to "answer if addressed as 'boy'" by "patrolmen bent on having some fun" (18). For he had endured the same treatment as a recently-discharged Naval officer in 1946, when he was stopped by Tennessee patrolmen and grilled about his dancing skill. (Chuck Berry asserts in his autobiography that in the early fifties black couples stopped by Missouri police were often forced to take antibiotic shots for venereal disease [90].)

In these books, however, the police are merely ambassadors of a larger menace that warps the mental trajectory of black travelers until pastoral nature, that enduring and conventional consolation of white travelers, and the typically neutral and prosthetic automobile often slough their healing powers and assume forbidding shapes.

In his hitchhiking interludes Griffin oscillates between pastoral and naturalistic depictions of nature as his situation changes. When he is trapped in a pickup with a sinister Alabama redneck who taunts him in a "voice unctuous with pleasure and cruelty," the landscape is Gothic:

> The highway stretched deserted through the swamp forests. He nodded toward the solid wall of brush flying past our windows.
> "You can kill a nigger and toss him into that swamp and no one'll ever know what happened to him." . . . he pulled off the main highway and stopped on a dirt road that led into the jungle. . . . "This is where I turn off. I guess you'll want to stick to the highway." (102)

When Griffin is safely out of the pickup, however, the Gothic gives way to a benign, lyrically invoked nature: "The woods issued no sound. I felt strangely safe, isolated, alone in the stillness of dusk turning to night. First stars appeared in darkening skies still pale" (103). After he is lovingly taken in by a poor black backwoods family the same night, Griffin reverts to the Gothic to frame their economic and spiritual isolation:

> And yet misery was the burden, the pervading, killing burden. . . . These moments of night when the swamp and darkness surrounded them evoked an immense loneliness, a dread, a sense of exile from the rest of humanity. . . . The [husband and wife's] union is momentary escape from the swamp night, from utter hopelessness of its ever getting better for them. (109–10).

For Griffin as for the other writers considered here, nature must be construed in racial terms—as a cover for racial crime, as a place to hide from violent white men, as a desolate retreat for subsistence living. Thoreau's famous boast that he was never burnt by owning the land he imaginatively possessed has often been taken up by white travelers who share with him the understanding that they could, after all, own the land. Thoreau, in the same passage, alluded to Alexander Selkirk, the model for Defoe's Robinson Crusoe, who was indeed monarch of all he surveyed. Chet Fuller's "deep travel" in the South—his off-road sojourns in North Carolina and Georgia in the late 1970s—brought him face to face with victims of rack-rent, real estate fraud, and abused labor. Such genteel and systemic oppression, running much deeper than the flagrant bigotry of earlier generations, led him to conclude that "Economics is *money* is *power* is *white*. . . . Whites, through their economic might, their control over the means of production in this country, still have the power to strangle us or let us breathe" (97). In America the traveling imagination is undeniably covetous. But when most of nature cannot be owned by African Americans, and when its white owners point to it as a place to secret castrated bodies, then imaginative possession, with all its pastoral delights, becomes an absurd delusion.

In the South, Williams found "the lovely scenery" to be "a mocking set behind which even the crimes of Hitler and his men, if one is to consider the number of people and the psychic damage involved, grow pale" (43). The contemplative pattern of Romantic road books disappears in *This Is My Country Too* as landscape winds inexorably back into labor and estrangement. The powdery earth and distant shade margins of Delta fields give way to "cotton fields, Negroes pulling long gunnysacks" (81). Or natural description dissolves into paranoia: "Above, the sky held blue. It was colder now, but the drought continued. I edged through the dangerous towns, tired but somehow hyperalert, seeing what wasn't always there and hearing what was without sound" (81). Harris saw in the clouds above the highway "no swans . . . no faces of dead presidents," but "hooded men dressed like angels in flowing white robes" (41).

The Transcendental business of rehabilitating the self must certainly begin with recognizing political and material checks on subjective freedom, as asserted by Emerson in "Self-Reliance" and "Politics" and Thoreau in "Resistance to Civil Government" and *Walden*. Both argued that property, social convention, and the state drove a wedge between "pure" nature and the independent self so that nature came to represent false abstractions such as ownership, power, and jurisdiction. When that happened, nature lost its organic power to represent moral truths and produced instead, as Emerson argued in *Nature*, a counterfeit moral language. In Williams's case those "false" abstractions can't be stripped away by an act of intellectual will because they wield an ineradicable material force. In yet another reversal of terms, pastoral nature—the Transcendentalists' "true" nature—becomes for Williams the *counterfeit* phenomenon, while nature bearing the signs of ownership and jurisdiction is genuine. Whereas the Transcendentalists celebrated the active power of imagination as a faculty Thoreau called a "realometer" (because it produced real moral vision as distinct from specious legal fictions), most of these black road writers dread and sometimes distrust what they imagine.

That imaginative vision usually summons a grotesque parallel universe, sometimes dangerous and delusional, as in the cases of Fuller's garage fantasy and many of Harris's encounters, and sometimes all the more jarring because its shadows are real. By the same token, the traveler may instinctively like the looks of a place, only to have his impression spoiled by evidence of its racial undertow. For example, at first blush Fuller was drawn to the old sector of Wilmington, North Carolina, its "quaint bars and shops like relics from waterfront towns of bygone years" (84). So far so good—Wilmington is another one of J. R. Humphreys' American Brigadoons: a charming nook untainted by history, just waiting to be rediscovered by a modern motorist. But the first black citizen Fuller talks up breaks the spell: "'Beautiful, my ass. . . . This is a racist town, brother. . . . It might look pretty from the outside, but it's some nasty shit going down here.'" In the end Fuller finds that he is "an outsider, a stranger with no invitation" (84).

Just as material social forces balk the Transcendental impulse in these narratives, the automobile's physical and mechanical attributes displace its epistemological function. There is a history of this emphasis in proletarian road narratives such as *The Grapes of Wrath* and *Rough Neck*, in which Steinbeck and Thompson devote long passages to breakdowns and repair as a way of contrasting refugee travel with pleasure touring. At the most basic level, exemplified by Fuller's breakdown in North Carolina, a malfunction robs the black driver of his protective anonymity and pitches him into the uncertain sphere of local service. Williams depended on his new car to provide a reliable "vault of safety" in the South (87). But even if it proved a reliable machine, its power posed a threat on yet another front:

Williams had to "get that big, fat motor to simmer down, behave itself, and keep me out of jail" (72). While Dallas Lore Sharp, echoing many another white traveler, exulted in a mystical union with his automobile on the plains of Kansas, Williams *feared* such a union, because if the machine should betray his impulses, if he could not govern either his body or his car, the state would imprison him. Insofar as race impounds the traveler, it defines the machine: desire, impulse, escape—the traditional automotive associations—must give way to restraint and conformity, those old Transcendental bugaboos. Only Harris, mounting his new BMW twelve years after Fuller drove a junker south, flaunts the speed of his machine.

In place of Dreiser's pastoral dream machine or the cowboy's horse to which Henry James implicitly likened the automobile, Williams's fantasy vehicle, recalled from his youth, is a war wagon: "After every reported lynching I saw myself in a specially made car. . . . Built into the front of the car were three machine guns, two .30 caliber and one .50. . . . The car, of course, was bulletproof, and . . . nothing on the road could catch us" (60). Contrast this with William Saroyan's paean in *Short Drive, Sweet Chariot*, published in 1966, a year after Williams's book: "The thing that was best was being free, and I had known this best thing most deeply when I had been in my own car on a long drive. I had known this freedom in myself most memorably, most unforgettably, getting into my own car, going, and not stopping until I felt like it" (111).

These counterpoised passages epitomize the contrary attitudes of black and white travelers toward space, machine, and self. Saroyan erases the machine and equates space with freedom; both license whim (one of Emerson's beloved terms) and enlarge the scope of desire. The "long drive" suggests an absence of resistance, much less danger. Williams, on the other hand, while still viewing the car as a projection of himself, morphs it until its latent armor and weaponry bristle. The driver bunkers in. He withdraws into the "vault of safety," his movement across the land a practical matter of superior speed and firepower. The car no longer shrinks into a cinematic dolly that tracks the eye through landscape; it swells to envelop the driver, protecting his *body*. There seems to be no question of conquest here, and certainly no reliving the discovery and subjugation of the land. Williams is historically alienated from that fantasy. Instead he draws on a *defensive* fantasy in which he resists—in the present—an historical force that has not been spent on the frontier, but continues to bear down on those it has not yet subjugated.

As you will recall, two years before Williams's 1963 trip, John Humphreys had compared the automobile to a time machine that spirited the traveler to colorful and mythic vestiges of America's past. This metaphor, which is implicitly adopted by many white travelers, figuratively sets the traveler outside history and renders history static and consumable, the sum of its charming appearances. The present is just movement and nostalgia, a "neutral" vantage whose only meaning lies in the endless duplication of a personal manifest destiny. Small wonder that a new generation of visitors from Europe still loves the old chestnut that America (in Baudrillard's version) "lives in a perpetual present" (76). While there are varying degrees of historical understanding among white travelers— enough at any rate to make Baudrillard's charge seem glib—these African American travelers cannot disentangle the present from the past or view Eco's historical simulacra as relics of a closed and harmless time.

Precisely because the American road has treated black travelers badly, among other things denying them the essential Transcendental prerequisite—the illusion of an expansive, omnipotent self—their personal crises and reckonings (Harris's sometimes excepted) do not have to be manufactured for the occasion, forced into a symbolic or philosophical artifice built up around the trip. The spirit-trying moments in these five books belong to a different order than even the most anguished passages of *Zen* or *Going Away*, and it is fitting they should occur haphazardly, as shocks. There are no epiphanies here.

Williams sometimes registers such episodes in world-weary understatement, as when, driving through North Dakota, he "suddenly tired of it all, the grins, the double takes. One man, his car filled with children, turned to grin and point at me. His car suddenly spurted dust as it veered off the narrow road. I watched him in the rear-view mirror as he skidded back on the highway, and I felt nothing for him or for the kids, not hate, not joy" (95–96). In transcontinental highway books—even in nineteenth-century travel accounts, like Irving's *A Tour on the Prairies*—the plains typically diminish the importance of the self and make travelers feel insignificant, if not frightened by their sublime desolation. In yet another reversal of conventions, this one geographical, the plains in Williams' narrative vanish; human conflict crowds out all margins of escape. Instead of a small capsule of privacy, or a prosthetic of consciousness, or even a vault of safety, the automobile becomes a sideshow for japing bigots—public and transparent but at the same time confining. There is something of the freak's stoicism in Williams's voice, both knowing and longsuffering, jaded by ridicule, so that the horror of his alienation is made keener by his apathy.

Fuller, by contrast, recounts crises with unrelieved vehemence. As a result, he spreads his emotion too thin and forfeits the effective climaxes that Rowan, Griffin, and Willliams achieved with more restraint and eloquence. His predecessors, however, were constrained by the decorum imposed by a white readership in ways Fuller was not. Williams, for example, was blasted in one review for, of all things, betraying a twinge of bitterness (Bernstein 143). Almost twenty years later, Fuller wrote in a different climate, one in which bitterness was fairly expected. And so I suspect that Fuller wrote what Rowan and Williams felt but could not express. What Fuller loses in grace, he more than wins back with candor.

The darkest moment in *I Hear Them Calling My Name* does not involve an indignity on the road, but Fuller's homecoming, to a comfortable Atlanta suburb. He has sojourned among the rural African American poor in North Carolina and Georgia, and he has traveled incognito as a poor laborer himself. Most recently he has befriended a Georgia man, Alan Chester, whose pay was docked when his white boss discovered he had bought a house, forcing Chester to quit that job and work two others, sleeping only on weekends. The memory of many such victims of white exploitation haunts Fuller's much anticipated "escape" into his own comparatively privileged world:

The next day, to celebrate my homecoming, we fired up the gas grill in the back yard, put ribs and chicken on to cook. . . .

We sat down to eat. That's when it happened.

The meat stuck in my throat like a wad of bandages. I thought I was going to choke. I jumped up heaving for breath. . . .

The storybook perfection was gone, shattered in an instant. Chills swept over me. . . . I thought my head would burst like a ripe melon and splatter all over the patio.

Then the pain was gone as quickly as it had come, and I plopped down, tired and scared. A depression like heavy black mud settled down on me, for I knew what was wrong. . . .

I did not want to face the poor anymore. . . .

I was tired of playing the game of being poor. It had made me feel sick. It had made me feel guilty. . . . I understood just how far behind I had left all the poor people I'd met in the months I'd been on the road. (149–50)

Clearly Fuller's sickening sense of his own privilege has led him to identify with the oppressors he has met or learned of in his travels. His journeys have confirmed that while casual and incidental racial prejudice is alive and well in the late seventies, systemic economic racism, perpetuated by moneyed interests—in textile mills, lumber yards, or real estate—inflicts deeper harm. His own wealth, modest as it may be, separates him from the have-nots with whom he has felt a racial kinship made more intense by his recent experiences as a menial hand. And so in concluding that class envy—inspired by a widening rift between the comfortable and the poor—more often crosses racial lines and turns blacks against one another, Fuller sees himself as a stranger to his own cause.

I can think of no other highway book in which the author admits to such uncertainty about the purpose and meaning of his journey and none in which the author so candidly offers up his anxiety, foolishness, and ambivalence at so many turns. He has sacrificed the conventional "strong" and self-possessed narrator who sorts and orders events and perceptions, and in the bargain he has risked harsh judgment from his readers—all in the interest of faithfully logging his responses, even at his own expense. If Fuller's style is at times swollen and clumsy, his tone jarringly fevered, he achieves a spontaneity and a frank humility that richly complicate the racial issues of his book. *I Hear Them Calling My Name* firmly rejects most conventional postures of self-discovery on the road while it offers one of the finest examples of how the road can yield up, not colorful or eccentric people, but lives that genuinely challenge the traveler's sense of self.

Eddy Harris ratchets Fuller's internalized anger into confrontation—with reader as well as Southern citizen. *South of Haunted Dreams* opens with a chronicle of famous racist hate crimes in the South and a quick dismissal of John Howard Griffin, whom Fuller had considered a civil rights pioneer. Griffin "told all about it in his book *Black Like Me*," Harris says, "But he could never really know it. He could never be black like me" (31–32). Drawing parallels between Ellison's *Invisible Man* and himself, Harris recounts the genesis of his blustering travel persona, tracing first his "colonization" in privileged, largely white education and society, then his revolt against acculturation and his adoption of a fierce racist identity. In the course of his journey, though, he talks with a number of thoughtful, sympathetic whites, and he decides that he has given in to racism prematurely: "I could see how through my surrender I had come to affirm and legitimize racism. I had lost myself to its addiction" (189). He admits that he "wanted to hate [the South]. . . . wanted the South to prove the stereotypes carefully harbored in my mind" (219). But in the end he "fell in love" with the region and its people (213), so that when he finally meets his bigot (after looking for him pretty hard), he can laugh off the encounter.

The general shape of *South of Haunted Dreams* reverses the pattern of increasing race consciousness found in the designs of other African American road books, yet it does so fitfully, as Harris swings from indignation to sentiment to rage. His assurance at times verges on self-aggrandizement, and his passionate observations frequently lapse into posturing and redundancy. But his brash persona is arguably a courageous response to keen racial embarrassments Harris has suffered before the trip.

The pivotal episode of John Howard Griffin's *Black Like Me* could not have occurred in any book by a black writer (as Harris makes plain), yet it changes utterly how we read those books. In Montgomery, Griffin decides to pass back into white society. He waits for the pigmenting drug to wear off, then scrubs off his superficial dye. Because he can't be seen as a white man leaving a black house, he waits until late at night to do so. When he does leave, he unintentionally threatens a black youth, who draws a switchblade:

> A policeman strolled toward us and the boy quickly dropped his weapon into his jacket pocket.
>
> The policeman nodded affably to me and I knew then that I had successfully passed back into white society, that I was once more a first-class citizen, that all doors into cafes, rest rooms, libraries, movies, concerts, schools and churches were suddenly open to me. After so long I could not adjust to it. A sense of exultant liberation flooded through me. I crossed over to a restaurant and entered. I took a seat beside white men at the counter and the waitress smiled at me. It was a miracle. . . . I saw smiles, benign faces, courtesies — a side of the white man I had not seen in weeks, but I remembered too well the other side. The miracle was sour. (119)

Griffin is our only travel writer who can speak from experience of the difference between journeying as a white man and journeying as a black man. The privilege of shucking his blackness necessarily lies behind his narrative as a proviso, despite the considerable costs he paid for writing his book. In the euphoria of his release, in the detailed catalogue of regained privileges, he supplies the suppressed texts of black travelers who cannot escape their blackness, who must concoct a distanced dignity (like Rowan) or a tired wisdom (like Williams) to shape their despair into some semblance of hope, or like Fuller, chronicle a furious bafflement at the web of economic and racial tensions that admit of few solutions.

Griffin undeniably proved his point, that racial prejudice existed in America, and he paid for it. His parents fled the country for Mexico, and he was forced to move his family out of Mansfield, Texas, to protect them from violence. Fuller, who appreciated both Griffin's sacrifice and the shock he delivered to a complacent white America in the early sixties, viewed his own book as a sequel to *Black Like Me*. "I was glad John Howard Griffin had gone before me," Fuller wrote, "because the effect his journey had on the hearts and minds of people in this country, blacks and whites, was making my job a little easier" (13).

The narratives of these five writers are different in kind from other American road books. They are not about escape from routine. They do not indulge in historical nostalgia. They do not concern the pursuit of the ideal self. "Whim" is not printed on their spines. They do not feed on the pleasure of consuming. They are not sentimental. Not one of them contains a map. Maps are about space and movement, other places, different ways, conquest, distance, space, novelty. And they do not, with the exception of Harris, deal in faddish angst or eloquent self-pity.

They do reveal the fraudulence of space viewed as an essence, transcending class and color. They do prove that travel writing can cause trouble, that it can expose social injustice and make people mad. They do bare the privileges white travelers take for granted. Most importantly, they engage the historical forces that produce them and resist all utopian fantasies predicated on the virtues of elsewhere.

Romances of the Road:

Seven Novels

5

Generally speaking, road trips in novels isolate, simplify, and magnify character. They serve the same purpose as Melville's fictive voyages, which incubate the mania or tenderness or courage of his sailors. In so doing, highway novels also reduce social static and push characters into more elemental conflicts with themselves, the American landscape, and the distanced claims of domesticity than they might experience at home. Obviously all these conditions are affected by the myth of Western space, and in this sense they are contrived and "false." But they operate no less powerfully for it.

In some road romances, usually older ones, the highway serves the domestic ideal by schooling and refining men and women to make them fit for their spouses. In the course of their adventures these travelers discover class prejudices as well as personal strengths and weaknesses, and they struggle against flaw and station to deserve the love of their desired objects. In other novels the highway undermines the domestic ideal by pitting the vitality of picaresque life against the dullness of permanent attachment. The claims of self-fulfillment or independence supersede the claims of marital bliss, though freedom, which seldom contents the protagonist, ultimately resolves nothing. In still others, the road provides a stage for grand self-destruction when neither domesticity nor vagabondage can appease the protagonist. Thomas and Agnes Wilby's *On the Trail to Sunset* (1912) and Sinclair Lewis's *Free Air* (1919) exemplify the first sort of novel. They adapt conventions from both the dime Western and the domestic courtship romance, complicating the course of true love with frontier perils. In both cases, Eastern characters (a man in *Sunset*, a woman in *Free Air*) are tested and tempered by Western nature and character types, thus fitting them for marriage in the end. And both novels depend upon a familiar symbolic polarity: in the East, conformity, routine and complacency prevail; in the West, self-reliance, adaptability, action, and nerve.

On the Trail to Sunset, much the cruder effort, is likely an embellishment of a 1911 motor trip chronicled in *Sunset Magazine* the next year (Eubank; Bliss 12). Both share the same itinerary, New York to San Diego by way of Chicago and Santa Fe, and the novel is illustrated with photographs of motorists in the West, roughly doctored to represent fictional events. Also, the fictional trip is launched amid the press hubbub over "Transcontinentalism" (24) and with fevered attention to outfitting (axes, spades, block and tackle, snakebite kit) (26) characteristic of early nonfiction accounts like that of Emily Post.

As *Sunset* opens, John Eastcott, a well-to-do man of New York society, decides to drive his nephew, Winthrop Hammond, out West to pick up Hammond's sweetheart, Evelyn Deering, in Chicago and conduct her to New Mexico, where her father is a wealthy rancher. When Eastcott's wife Nora finds she is to be left out of the party, she protests, "am I just a 'Norah,' to be left behind in my 'Doll's House' when there's a little hardship to be endured?" (11). She does nonetheless chafe at having her "lovely parties and musicales sacrificed on the altar of a stupid motor car!" (11).

In Chicago the Eastcotts and Hammond discover that Evelyn has fallen prey to the charms of Emilio Santo, a sinister but winsome Hispanic revolutionary who is plotting the secession of New Mexico and Arizona. Santo's coarse virility makes him a suitable native rival and foil for Hammond, just appealing enough to a woman of the rugged Southwest, but unlike Hammond, violent, duplicitous, and racially tainted (the narrator calls him a "greaser"). In the course of the journey along the old Santa Fe Trail, Hammond braves car chases and gunplay, proving his fitness to wed the tough Anglo girl of the Southwest.

The plot of *On the Trail to Sunset* is a preposterous throwback, and its reactionary colonialism, depicting Hispanics as wild-eyed fanatics and Native Americans as childish, defeated savages, lacks the revisionist romanticism of later nonfiction narratives, apparently because in the Wilbys' eyes Anglo conquest remains to be finished by the likes of Winthrop Hammond. He must first learn how to be "simple and direct" like Evelyn Deering—"what the West really means"—before he can do so, and his adventures teach him how to do it (146). Evelyn's father, Colonel (of course) Deering, assures him that "if you want to live as men should live, you can do it better here than in New York" (253). Winthrop's marriage to Evelyn shows that a cultivated Easterner tempered in the elemental Southwest can muster virility enough to better his native rival without shedding his manners, thus insuring the right and proper march of Anglo civilization into the recesses of the continent.

Like *Sunset*, Sinclair Lewis's *Free Air* is an episodic automotive romance that shares a factual itinerary, in this case Lewis's transcontinental journey with his wife, Grace Hegger Lewis, in 1916. (The newly married couple drove from Minnesota to the Pacific Northwest in a Model T Ford.) And like the Wilbys' novel, *Free Air* centers on lovers from very different walks of life. Lewis's Claire Boltwood is a Brooklyn Heights socialite and Milt Daggett is a Schoenstrom, Minnesota, auto mechanic. Both books thrust regional and class tensions between the lovers, both feature education by immersion in the West, and both end in a marriage. But even so early in his career, before the great novels of the twenties— *Main Street, Babbitt, Elmer Gantry*—Lewis commanded a much richer and subtler talent for realizing and then juxtaposing classes and regional cultures. *Free Air* builds a more elaborate and layered contrast between urban high society and Western entrepreneurship than *Sunset*. As a result the regional conflict worked out through its lover-representatives, while still contrived, generates a good deal more ambiguity because it depends less on caricatures to propel the action.

Claire Boltwood interrupts her "gracious leisure" in Brooklyn Heights to chauffeur her overworked father, Henry Boltwood, from Minneapolis (where their car is shipped from New York) across the high plains to the home of wealthy cousins, the Gilsons, in Seattle. As the Wilbys also tell us, transcontinental motoring was touted, in the teens, as a balm for exhaustion, and Claire bullies her father, who has predictably suffered "nervous prostration" in the railroad business, into such a regimen (13). Taking leave of "mansions like mausoleums," "foundries and shipyards," Claire assumes the wheel and launches her "voyage into democracy" (10, 45). She very soon gets what she wants—"something to struggle against"—in the sloughs disguised as roads in rural Minnesota, which consume all her strength and attention. She is also delighted to discover that "there's people in the world who want to know us without having looked us up in the Social Register!" (45–46).

Though gritty and independent, Claire soon requires the aid of the mechanic Daggett, who leaves the considerable business he has built in Schoenstrom to shadow the Boltwoods westward as a guardian. In his dependable but humble Teal "bug," Milt keeps out of sight until his services are required; then he materializes to get them out of a jam. Milt's reticence gradually wins him Claire's trust, and when he drubs a lecher who attempts to hijack the Boltwoods, the romance is on its way.

And so is Lewis's highway dialectic. His Western character—brave, resourceful, kind, and mechanically gifted—is good raw stuff, but as he comes to know Claire on the road he learns that to court her properly he must refine his taste and manners and educate himself in the arts. To accomplish the first, he looks to traveling salesmen ("drummers") who know "the good things" and thus can show him "how to perform the miracle of changing from an ambitious boy into what Claire would recognize as a charming man" (87). Milt embarks on his further education by reading books Claire has given him, including Vachel Lindsay's *The Congo* (1914). Here he discovers "manly" writers more suited to his temperament than the "Old Boys" of Europe with their "rhymed belly-achin' about hard luck" (98). Lewis's Eastern character—refined, leisured, urbane—must detach herself, on the road, from the "limousinvalids, insulated from life by plate glass," and the "smug tourists" on the train, who are, as she once was, estranged from the common people: the "sagebrush tourists," telephone linemen, and work crews (120–21, 243). Claire's voyage into democracy teaches her that these are "her own people," and that the "Real West" is "hers, since she had won to it by her own plodding" (122–23).

From time to time foil characters appear from Claire's and Milt's past to tempt them back to the extremes of the original antitheses, but these are safely overcome. By the time they reach Seattle, Claire can with some regret cast off the aristocratic Gilsons, who "shut out the common world" (247), and Milt can finish his climb by studying French, attending concerts and lectures, and lifting weights—all while he completes his mechanical engineering degree. Claire confesses to Milt, "I'm a thoroughly ignorant parasite woman" and begs him to "make me become real! A real woman!" (239). That he does. In the end the synthesis (Milt's proposal) is catalyzed by another road trip, in a new Teal bug: "Firs dashing by—rocks in the sunshine—clouds jaunty beyond the inviting mouth of a mountain pass—even the ruts and bumps and culverts—she seemed a part of them all. In the Gilsons' huge cars she had been shut off from the road, but in this tiny bug, so close to the earth, she recovered the feeling of struggle, of triumph over difficulties, of freedom unbounded. And she could be herself" (364–65).

Even so early in the road book's history, *Free Air* broaches most of its pervasive themes. It directs the forces of Western space, automotive independence, democratic sentiment, and Transcendental individualism to a domestic end, so that freedom means shedding the unnecessary constraints of any narrow society in America in order to possess a mate whose essence is desirable. Recreational automobile travel, in its movement away from fixed society, frees this essence and in doing so breaks down class barriers that separate not only potential mates, but everyone else. Frank Capra's film *It Happened One Night* (1934) shows the automotive picaresque widening its influence in the same way, first joining lovers from different classes and then uniting a busload of people from all walks of life in a rousing chorus of "The Man on the Flying Trapeze."

Such is the case in numerous kin-trip nonfiction books written before the fifties. But in many later road novels and nonfiction narratives, marriage and family become constraints instead of ends. Indeed, even the nonfiction women's books *Westward Hoboes* and *A Long Way from Boston* feature distinctly nondomestic, gender-challenging themes, looking forward to the antidomestic male picaresque so common in both fiction and nonfiction road books after midcentury.

Along with Sigal's *Going Away*, Kerouac's *On the Road* and Douglas Woolf's sadly overlooked *Wall to Wall* (1962) herald the arrival of the antihero vagabonds—trucking coast to coast, superheated by despair, running scared, skirting the mantraps of America. Like the classic picaro, they are not likely to change, but unlike him, they are painfully self-conscious and quite aware of their historical situation, particularly the fevered postwar rush to domesticity. The roots of the type can be found in Hemingway's unmoored men, in the canny amoral characters of Raymond Chandler, James M. Cain (who resented the term "hardboiled"), and Jim Thompson, and in the variously principled drifters of B. Traven.

Both *Wall to Wall* and *On the Road* narrate events from a decade or so before, postdating a sensibility from the late forties and early fifties. Woolf's book is the more accomplished, in its crisp, oblique prose and tightly maneuvered encounters, while Kerouac's is the more charismatic—quick, accidental, automatic. Erotically the novels are heterosexual, but women no longer complete the novels' male characters. The complementary educations of future mates on the road are jettisoned as women come to be sessile creatures, at best earth-mothery comforters or clever fetching lays, at worst bogs of motherhood and harbingers of duty and routine. In short, women are absorbed into the old binary scheme, allied with consumption along the road, production at road's end. Most often they are associated with the threat of reproduction in every sense.

Wall to Wall follows the peregrinations of Claude Squires as he leaves his father and sister and a dead-end job as a "Helper II" in a state madhouse in Los Angeles, crosses the country in two drive-away cars, and briefly visits his paranoid mother in a Boston asylum. Along the way he sleeps with two women, Vivien James and Fran Jones, both old acquaintances.

Every domestic situation in the book reeks of bitterness and despair, if not insanity, more or less reflecting Claude's own childhood, split between the homes of an alcoholic, womanizing father and a deranged mother. He and his sister were "fired back and forth, like tennis balls put by for weekend use—served up overhand but with a twist in hope that the receiver would flub his shot." This shuttling took place in his father's car, at breakneck speed, "over the countryside which we were too low down and blacked out to see" (116). These harrowing rides barely gave the children time to recover from their sadness at leaving one parent and put on cheerful faces for the other. With this kind of start it isn't surprising that Claude, at twenty-five, associates the highway with loss and anticipation, which he in turn associates with sexual relations. Indeed, the novel's plot repeats the pattern of his childhood, a movement from coast to coast, from father to mother. By this point, however, his father has spent his lust and become a pathetic fundamentalist, and his mother has gone mad. Since the families Claude encounters on the road are neither better nor worse than his own, he is left the shuttle itself, source of his keenest familial emotions. "The funny thing is," he tells Vivien, "I still like upheaval for upheaval's sake" (116).

Claude's journey replays the escape loop many times over, and the escapee is always recaptured by his or her past. Claude is a poor accomplice, for obvious reasons. The pattern is comically rendered in Claude's numerous attempts to smuggle a recidivist wetback from Sonora into Arizona. Pete is always promptly sprung from Claude's trunk and sent home. With Claude's liaisons, especially Vivien, the motif assumes a darker cast.

Though only twenty, Vivien has put her drunken brother through engineering school and still runs what amounts to a hospice for him and their invalid mother. "I want to get out of here!" she tells Claude, and she wants him to take her (98). After their brief sojourn in a desolate hotel in Perhaps and a camping interlude, he puts her on notice that he is not ready to marry: "I'm still a tramp. For all I know I may always be. I'm afraid you think that going to bed with a man changes him, some dream like that. It isn't true. . . . I don't seem to be able to make up my mind whether I'm telling you off or seducing you" (100). Vivien's own remorse about leaving her charges abets Claude's honesty, and in the end they part on the good terms only road fiction knows, though Claude again experiences the "suicidal pangs that any parting left him with" (86). Fran Jones likewise wants to flee her diner life with him, but her long years as a working divorcee have fortunately toughened her against likely disappointment. Thus in good consumer fashion Claude leaves his lovers as he had left his sister in Los Angeles, "as though he were leaving a store with something he had bought in another store earlier, before he remembered they also carried it here" (31).

Wall to Wall nullifies every version of domesticity. It does not do so capriciously, because the protagonist's character is spoiled by a riven childhood. Neither does it sacrifice domesticity to its opposite, unfettered road joy, because Claude's road is always that of the emotional refugee. Malaise and poor rearing, however, can't veil the book's overriding heterosexual male fantasy, for all the cushioning self-pity. Woolf's exculpatory strategy in the end fails to mask the essential desire to fuck and book down the road, to spurn entanglement. That desire, formulaically impossible even for the crusty realist Sinclair Lewis in 1919, registers over the weakest psychic protests by the middle of the century.

On the Road is a novel of little households and big highways. Sal Paradise meets Dean Moriarty soon after Sal has split from his wife. The breakup has afflicted him with a "serious illness" caused by a "feeling that everything was dead" (3). This illness, like Claude's suicidal pangs, is a familiar kind of trumped-up remorse the novelist can play when his character might be suspected of having no soul—it's the TV cop who vomits when he has to kill someone. It is also, I think, a vestige of the old domestic romance, a twinge that dies hard, even in novels of rebellion against the postwar nesting frenzy. While the road trips in Kerouac's novel career away from the little households, they move toward them, too, in a kind of dizzy circularity. Without the cachet of those households, drifters risk being seen as bums, or worse, impotent or asexual or homosexual bums. Households, however they may stifle the male spirit, stick as holdovers of middle-class expectations, vestigial but necessary ingredients in the definition of manhood.

Sal's proletarian tent household with Terry during his migrant cotton-picking experiment thrills him with its rustic charm: "There were a bed, a stove, and a cracked mirror hanging from a pole; it was delightful. I had to stoop to get in, and when I did there was my baby and my baby boy" (94). Sal discovers that he is "a man of the earth, precisely as I had dreamed I would be, in Paterson" (97). One page later, however, he feels not the romance of the earth, but "the pull of my own life calling me back" (98). And then, "well, Lackadaddy, I was on the road again" (101). Having lived a hard life in the fields, Terry understands Sal's wanderlust, and she gives him back to the road.

Dean shares Marylou with Sal in San Francisco, but according to both Sal and Dean she is a whore, and thus easily shucked. Camille, Dean's next girlfriend, is in Sal's view "a relief after Marylou; a well-bred polite young woman" (174). Yet when Sal returns to San Francisco and finds Camille raging and pregnant with Dean's second child, Sal professes to have "no idea what was really wrong" (183). His idiotic naivete, opening the episode in which his loyalty to Dean gets its biggest test, establishes the grounds for excusing Dean in the end: "by virtue of his enormous series of sins, [he] was becoming the Idiot, the Imbecile, the Saint of the lot" (193). Because holy idiocy will not quite subdue the faint twitch of domestic sentiment, Kerouac is tasked with belittling the women. The novel's logic does most of the work. Sal and Dean are Western heroes, Rattlesnake Bills—not by nature fathers—so Camille has been foolish to tempt Dean's nature in the first place. The inquisition at Galatea Dunkel's, after Dean has left Camille, finds him in the middle of the room, hounded by his female accusers. "It wasn't anything but a sewing circle," Sal says (193). Dean is able to walk away because, miraculously, the biddies too are transformed by his idiocy: "there was a strange sense of maternal satisfaction in the air, for the girls were really looking at Dean the way a mother looks at her dearest and most errant child" (195).

The fixed gender spheres of home and road do away with the more egalitarian possibility of highway courtship in the earlier novels. In *Free Air* Milt and Claire will have a home and children, but they are last seen enjoying each other's company on a Western drive. *On the Road* merely replays the adolescent's departure from home. This pattern demands that the men and women be viewed in different lights in different stages of their relationships. As the men approach and seduce women, they are hardy and tender and hungry rovers. Their objects are sweet and vulnerable. When it is time for the men to leave, their girls have become either whores or mothers, and they have become errant children. They must escape to the vitality of male companionship in space; the heterosexual courtship is displaced by a spiritually homosexual courtship of the sort made famous by Leslie Fiedler's *Love and Death in the American Novel*.

The incredibly conventional ending of *On the Road* marks a capitulation to the formal calculus of romantic comedy, in the sense that the two central male characters settle down with women, but it does not effectively challenge the picaresque assault on domesticity that has ruled the book. Once again, the token reversion to domesticity is meant to assure us that Sal and Dean are not brutish vagabonds, but merely young men whose vigorous love of experience transcends the routine of home life as long as it must. Dean, whose soul is "wrapped up in a fast car, a coast to reach, and a woman at the end of the road," implausibly finds himself "settled with his most constant, most embittered, and best-knowing wife Camille" (230, 308). Sal discovers in Laura "the girl with the pure and innocent dear eyes that I had always searched for and for so long" (306). Unlike *Wall to Wall, On the Road* is a sentimental book through and through, which in itself cushions the implausibility of Kerouac's ending. But the book's sentiment is always transitory and neurotic. It dodges character. So the domestic resolution, while it shares in that sentiment, can't merge the separate spheres of men and women in a way that makes domesticity believably permanent. Woolf sensibly denies this resolution. Claude Squires obeys the logic of his character. He may always be a tramp.

Jim Harrison's *A Good Day to Die* (1973) is road noir in the tradition of *Wall to Wall*, yet it shares just a trace of *On the Road*'s pastoral energy, almost absent in Woolf's novel. The anonymous narrator is a staple antihero—an angry, sensitive ne'er-do-well given to turns of brutality and remorse, whose wit and self-knowledge sustain a measure of appeal. He has left his wife and daughter and retreated from "urban life" and from work, which makes him "vomit a lot," to find solace in "the 'land,'" fishing, and whiskey (93, 46, 92). In Key West he meets Tim, who is recovering from facial wounds suffered in Vietnam. They decide to drive to the Grand Canyon and dynamite a dam, whose rumored construction would flood the canyon. En route they pick up Sylvia, Tim's girlfriend, who in time divides her affections between the men. When the Arizona enterprise comes to naught, they drive to Idaho and, in a "fatuous" gesture, dynamite a small earthen dam that is impeding salmon cycles. Tim is killed in the blast. In the end the narrator overcomes his desire to care for Sylvia, and he nobly resolves to leave her.

A Good Day to Die marks the exhaustion of the Romantic possibilities of the American highway, and it does so by straining the myth, on its own terms, until it snaps. *Wall to Wall*, *Going Away*, and *On the Road* are wending toward this; the road's allure is becoming more deliberate and ironic. In this book the road West finally appears as an empty projection, leading not to a new self but to the same unchanging self.

The book's road trip is prompted by historical circumstances that promise to make the trip larger than its travelers. Tim has been disfigured in every way by the war. The West, according to the narrator, is being spoiled by "realtors, land developers, and lumber companies" (35). Since Tim and the narrator have nothing left to console them but the wilderness—where there is no civilization to snare them in war, work, or marriage—they embark on an eco-guerrilla mission à la Edward Abbey's Monkey Wrench Gang. This quixotic undertaking might galvanize these characters into redemptive insurgency, requiting Tim's bitterness and pulling the narrator out of his funk. But the road trip can't bear the weight of its symbolic importance to them. Tim's amphetamine-gulping, maniacal driving and constant desire to blow up things just for the sport reduce the whole enterprise to an empty gesture rendered more absurd by his death. The narrator, who at first looks to Tim as a way out, a fellow "goat" but one with purpose, is soon disillusioned by Tim's violence, a turn that flattens his own response to "the land" he had sought: "I was sated with the West. . . . I walked to the car in an utter numb boredom with forests, rivers, mountains, cars, Tim and Sylvia" (123).

The novel's bleak erotics, verging on misogyny, completely erase the domestic agenda. As her name implies, Sylvia, the central erotic object, is an unsophisticated "natural" creature, linked to wilderness pleasure. The course of her seduction by the narrator parallels the travelers' westward course, and the narrator's conquest and disappointment roughly coincide with his being "sated" by the West. Early on she rouses old passions in him: "the juice still seemed to be there, no matter how narrowed and atrophied. The delight in the air and water and trees and in such rare creatures as Sylvia" (56). But the sylvan creature has two handles, and only two. Within a week she has "a goddamn dumb hillbilly face," a "stupid cow brain." She's "beautiful," but she's "an out and out stupid cunt. Period" (102). Later he says "she was some hearth goddess who was sweet, virtuous, gentle, kind and faithful. . . . And she was simple-minded. . . . Tie her up and throw her over the cliff on the left side of the car" (131). The narrator claims to be an honest brute, helpless before his passions, trapped in a world he never made (131). A fair judgment, but transparently exculpatory. On one hand he knows that the land and the woman he seeks are fantasies that can be sustained only so long as he believes in their power to move him; he considers romanticism a disease. On the other, he yearns for the wilderness and a hearth goddess.

142

Even in the 1970s—a decade exceeding the legal limit for earth mothers, literary and otherwise—this character's desires are beset by a lethal triteness, as if they were conceived to be thwarted. And I think that is the case. *On the Road*, though it caved to waning domestic ideals in the end and bracketed the Western road in a prolonged but finite adolescence (as *The Dharma Bums*, in 1958, did not), had pushed both Western road flight and the hearth goddess very near the ironic edge ten years before. Harrison's narrator regresses, purposely reliving the same disappointments, but this time as an angry man outliving the wayward youth who could still be cowed by women. In fact, the narrator of *A Good Day to Die* despises women. He twice imagines murdering his female companion, the first before the end of the novel's prologue. In each instance the woman fails to act like a man. She can't fish or think or stand up to another man. The fact that he is drawn to such women, given to idealize the absence of manliness in them, suggests that he seeks the greatest threat to his independence—the virtuous cunt—in order to justify destroying it.

Near the end of the novel Sylvia and the narrator commemorate Chief Joseph's heroic but futile march toward Canada in 1877 by painting their faces and pretending to be Indians (167). The narrator had earlier pictured Sylvia as "a Nez Percé squaw ready to cook her brave's fish" but dismissed the vision as foolish romanticism (142). For all the disclaimers, such brittle historical romanticism, deflecting as it does the immediate human cost of this Western journey, ultimately nudges the highway romance beyond sentiment and irony into dark farce.

In *A Good Day to Die* the narrator's self-loathing grows out of long experience, which effectively diminishes its power to offset his thought and behavior. He claims to be a victim—of capitalism, domestic strictures, stupid women, land developers, and, most importantly, his own inescapable personality. Yet as the threats to his freedom pile up along the road, his victim's posture loses its hard-boiled charm, and its credibilty.

By contrast, the young female narrator of Katherine Dunn's *Truck* (1971), though she entertains equally violent fantasies of revenge against real and imaginary people who would imprison her in work or family, has not yet tested her personality, so her fantasies can be chalked up to *real* adolescence. The title is not a noun but the coined verb, which refers to the fifteen-year-old narrator, Dutch, leaving home for a life someplace in the wild where she can become invisible. In an opening fantasy vignette Dutch imagines herself naked in the forest, where *"nobody will own me anymore"* (1). She flees her home, because if she doesn't, she will "get a job in a supermarket and never nick anything. . . . Spend all my money on clothes and sit at night with Maw in front of the TV sewing on my hope chest and waiting for the right Flying A man to come along. Too much. Too much to stand. I really would end up killing somebody. Feeling the knife one day and red and anger and all the lost minutes and wasted hours come pouring out" (67).

Like the resourceful picara she is, Dutch steals and sells, hoards and schemes to prepare for her journey; like the daughter of all American adventurers, from Lewis and Clark and Thoreau to Emily Post, she outfits, cataloguing canteens, books, and fishhooks. On the first leg, to Los Angeles, on a bus, she recalls what she likes about the road: "When it's good in a car I never want to stop. Just keep going forever. The stopping makes me feel sick and tight like it's time to die. . . . just go on fast down the road" (82). She meets her friend Heydorf, a proudly amoral drifter, in L. A., where she at last feels "light and good and powerful. Invisible" (104). But all the time she fears that she will be drawn back, after her "little fling," and "marry a service station attendant and sit in a cozy fucking little house with a toaster bringing up sleazy brats and reading fancy books to forget I'm dead. I'll hate him. . . . I'll throw a pan of boiling water at him" (107).

Heydorf and Dutch make their way up the coast and eventually set up camp in a secluded inlet. In time he leaves her, is arrested for a beach murder and released, and joins the army. Dutch survives for a spell, surf fishing and grubbing, but the romantic wilderness life she has imagined soon erodes her courage and her body; emaciated and sick, she agrees to be taken to juvenile authorities. In the detention home she must "put on faces" once again, but she relishes food and warmth (198). Her mother roundly argues before the juvenile court that she should be allowed to return home—a defense Dutch admires—but when she is welcomed home with a wholesome picnic, she finds that she is "not theirs anymore: . . . I can remember caring and wanting and needing but I don't anymore" (210). She achieves her invisibility, at last, in her home. The novel concludes with Dutch's fantasizing that she has murdered the beach lovers Heydorf is accused of killing, thereby coolly avenging the loss of her conventional future and irrevocably foiling the claims of her society.

The conclusions of *A Good Day to Die* and *Truck* differ as their protagonists differ. One character flees kinship through space; the other, while materially dependent on her family, flees inward. But both books share a revulsion with domesticity that widens into a general hopelessness about life in America. In both cases the wilderness, that old Romantic standby, proves an empty thing. Flight can no longer dissipate the pent-up fears and anxieties produced at home or in the workplace. Instead the nomadic gesture is accompanied by violent and self-destructive fantasies and deeds. Fairly all the staple benefits of the highway touted in every genre of road book have disappeared in these novels—including the nondomestic spirit of independence voiced by early women motoring without men. Even the novel immediately anticipating these burnout books, *Going Away*, for all its narrator's galloping self-pity, builds an elaborate historical context—in the failure of organized labor, the political apathy of the suburbs, and the lapse of cultural ideals—as grounds for the narrator's discontent; moreover, he acts on his despair by leaving the country for good.

While the prospects of self-discovery on the road remain healthy in Anglo nonfiction of roughly the same period, how is it that the novel offers so many examples of violent despair? For one thing the imperatives of domestic monogamy are so rooted in the genre that rebellion against them demands an equal and opposite reaction, the annihilation of the rebel. For another, our sympathy for the male rebel is prepared by the Promethean and Satanic traditions stemming from the Romantic period, in which the subversive will and intellect, often embodied by a charismatic but "evil" character, challenge conventional ideas and behavior with tragic results. In the case of alienated women who withdraw from a patriarchal society in order to preserve an uncompromised identity, we have the tradition of the "madwoman in the attic" chronicled by Sandra Gilbert and Susan Gubar in their book by the same name. The postwar assault on suburban domesticity, as it is played out in road novels featuring erotic interests, merges all three formulas.

But the mannered coolness of Stephen Wright's 1994 *Going Native* estranges the novel's disaffected characters from even these patterns of rebellion. The rebellion stays put—the action begins with the protagonist leaving his family. But the motive has shifted from intrinsic disentanglement from a suffocating culture to a frantic, objectified pursuit of that culture. In *Going Native* the long-sublimated libido for novelty and consumption—a drive reconfigured, in these later burnout books, to elevate rebellion to existential pathos—is finally disclosed as a grim, almost naturalistic, determinism, taking the place of biological and psychoanalytical models of determinism that have come before. Here all the themes of a century's road books are deconstructed, flayed alive, in a pitiless treatment of absurd media-engendered yearning.

In an appropriately conventional opening sequence, Wylie Jones flees a depressing cocktail party in his Chicago house, heists a neighbor's old Galaxy, and hits the road for California. In subsequent tales, Jones, who adopts first the name of his friend Tom Hanna and then a variety of pseudonyms (including Wylie Coyote), reappears to complete action begun by new characters—a homicidal hitchhiker, a befuddled young couple on the run, a covey of pornographers, a lesbian couple, a hapless woman whom he marries, a Hollywood actress and director returning from Borneo, and finally a third wife and her child. Jones attempts to kill himself in the middle of the novel, fails, and thereafter turns murderer, killing his second wife, the Hollywood couple and their friends. Eventually Jones becomes a compulsive imposter, donning wigs, switching identities and license plates. In the end, in the home of his third wife, he dresses as a woman, then strips off his costume and shoots himself as he sits in the driver's seat of his green Galaxy.

Jones, like most of the people he encounters as he goes native in

America, is trying to still a raging boredom by dosing it with the homeopathic snakeoil of novelty. Every new experience or identity instantly becomes old, and the threshold of interest rises exponentially. Highway travel takes its place beside sex, music, advertisement, and murder as another fleeting occupation of the insatiable consciousness. In episode after episode, restless characters cast frantically about for entertainment. A young motel clerk Jones picks up in Colorado typifies Wright's American:

> Her mind a roiling inferno, Aeryl stalked the borders of the room, reviewing the well-tested chinks in the mortar, deciding where to sink the probe. . . . She raised the blinds. Beyond the cracked asphalt of the parking lot . . . stretched six straightaway lines of unrebuffed speed as familiar as the back of her hand and equally hypnotic, the fundamental lure of moving objects . . . the ever-thrilling possibility of accident, a splatter of color upon the surrounding monotone, a spray of primal drugs into bodily systems dulled by dullness. . . . She stepped to the television and changed the channel. . . . Skinny guys in tight leather were hopping up and down. . . . She jacked up the volume, settled back in her father's chair, held simultaneously by the battle of the demonic bands and the soulless shuttling of traffic at her window, fidgety eyes jumping from one screen to another, waiting for somebody cute to show up via either medium. No contest. Forty-five minutes of desk clerk duty had offered her the wrinkled potatoheads of enough fat truck drivers and balding husbands to cover a week's grossout. . . . The bloated ugliness of the land, candy-coated corn. (113)

Earlier road writers like Robertson, Pirsig, and Heat-Moon recognized and deplored driving as a hypnotic medium like television, while the Pranksters reversed the imperative and multiplied distracting stimuli. For or against the trend, all were aware that electronic media and automobiles were forging a new consciousness in America, one in which all experience would be judged against the hyperkinetic profusion of novelty generated by screen and speaker and windshield. No contest: how can the balding husbands compete with the TV punkers, "shaking their hair, their guitars, their buns, the stage wreathed in thunderheads of smoke pierced by multitudes of spots, dragon flames roaring from mortar tubes"? (113). Wylie Jones suffers the same

> unappeasable itch that worked without respite under his skin [and] seemed to believe it could find what it was seeking somewhere on that magical screen. But, typically, the more he watched, the more restless he became. He was helpless to stop. The same futile routine day after day, night after night. Click, click, click. He wanted to see something he hadn't seen before. . . . Out of the house and onto the road, a solitary in his cage, he joined the other solitaries locked and buckled into their cages, hundred, thousands of them, all streaming determinedly along in a credible masquerade of purpose and conviction. How many understood, as he did, the true function of the car as a secret device for finding yourself. (282)

That last statement roars down through the century, and here it hits a wall, for Wylie Jones has no self left. Self-discovery on the road, one of the culture's tantalizing promises, has become yet another of the "encoded cliches" issuing from "the media microwaves bombarding his skin" (282). He will soon be costumed, in red hair and mustache, as a bibliophile, and his car bears stolen plates; he has decided to cure his boredom with television by picking up and (possibly) murdering a bookstore clerk—but not before savoring the "garish spectacle of ranked identities" on the bookshelves (287). Desperately fighting "the ever-present danger of a forgetting deep and prolonged," trying "to remain clean by hosing himself off in the daily data stream," Jones finally dissolves into the media that have fashioned his various selves (287, 303). In the end, as he prepares to kill himself in the Galaxy, he discovers that going native in America meant "there was no you. There was only the Viewer, slumped in his sour seat, the bald shells of his eyes boiling in pictures" (305).

And so in this vein of road noir writing the fictional motoring self, by 1994, is spent—a casualty of its own promotional campaign. Beginning with *Wall to Wall*, and continuing through *Truck*, *A Good Day to Die*, and Jim Dodge's *Not Fade Away* (1987), theme and striking prose styles vie more and more forcefully with character until they virtually erase it in *Going Native*. Indeed, Wright's Pynchonesque virtuosity as a stylist all but drowns his human voices. In this quality he revisits the dark irony of Nathanael West or John Franklin Bardin. And when he shoulders out the clichés that have driven his characters, he scotches the characters, too; the result is that his people are interchangeable fools. It follows that erotic connections have shed all traces of sentiment and guilt, devolving into yet another unsatisfying medium. The children involved in Wylie Jones's first and third marriages appear only briefly—as lost and neglected figures—to foreshadow a new generation of scorched Viewers.

To be sure, though this genealogy of road romances traces an important line of descent from Sinclair Lewis to Stephen Wright, it passes over collateral versions, later narratives that do not follow the same grimly solipsistic path. Larry McMurtry's road erotics in *Moving On* and *Cadillac Jack*, for example, incline toward the nostalgic and sentimental, linking landscape (which matters less and less in the noir books) with genuine romantic attachments, however impermanent. And John Updike's Rabbit tetralogy creates a cycle in which Harry Angstrom's highway flights from domestic pain repeatedly draw him back into familial duty. But by and large the myth of discovering one's essence on the road has met its debunking, in fiction, as the century turns. In part this end has been brought about by the mass production of a myth in which the self must shun the duplication of products or ways of life. When one's hankering for fresh experience on the road sits up on the shelf like a can of corn, the traveler becomes an ironist to sublimate the cannery.

Still, although the consumer has become the main product of late capitalism, as Richard Godden puts it—the traveler's gesture of escape cunningly shaped by advertisers—the American road may yet be framed by something other than irony and parched rebellion and fashion: we may yet have stouter tales enriched by the sadness of place.

BIBLIOGRAPHY

Abbey, Edward. *The Monkey Wrench Gang*. 1975. New York: Avon, 1976.

Algren, Nelson. *A Walk on the Wild Side*. 1956. New York: Fawcett Crest, n.d.

Baudrillard, Jean. *America*. 1986. Trans. Chris Turner. London: Verso, 1988.

Beagle, Peter S. *I See by My Outfit*. 1965. New York: Penguin, 1985.

Beauvoir, Simone de. *America Day by Day*. 1948. Trans. Patrick Dudley. London: Duckworth, 1952.

Belasco, Warren. "Commercialized Nostalgia: The Origins of the Roadside Strip." *The Automobile and American Culture*. 1980. Ed. David L. Lewis and Laurence Goldstein. Ann Arbor: U of Michigan P, 1986. 105–22.

Belden, J. "Motoring in the High Sierras." *Scribner's* 57 (Feb. 1915): 201–13.

Bercovitch, Sacvan. *The American Jeremiad*. Madison: U of Wisconsin P, 1978.

Bernstein, A. H. Rev. of *This Is My Country Too*, by John A. Williams. *Bestseller* 25 (15 June 1965): 143, 147.

Berry, Chuck. *Chuck Berry: The Autobiography*. New York: Harmony, 1987.

Bliss, Carey S. *Autos across America: A Bibliography of Transcontinental Automobile Travel, 1903–1940*. Los Angeles: Dawson's, 1972.

Brinkley, Douglas. *The Majic Bus: An American Odyssey*. New York: Harcourt, 1993.

Bryson, Bill. *The Lost Continent: Travels in Small-Town America*. 1989. New York: HarperPerennial, 1990.

Caldwell, Erskine. *Around about America*. New York: Farrar, 1964.

Chatwin, Bruce. *The Songlines*. New York: Viking, 1987.

Clecak, Peter. *America's Quest for the Ideal Self*. New York: Oxford UP, 1983.

Crane, Stephen. *Maggie: A Girl of the Streets*. New York, 1893.

Crevecoeur, Hector St. John De. *Letters from an American Farmer*. 1782. *Letters from an American Farmer and Sketches of Eighteenth Century America*. Ed. Albert Stone. New York: Penguin, 1986.

Daniels, Jonathan. *A Southerner Discovers the South*. New York: Macmillan, 1938.

Dettelbach, Cynthia Golomb. *In the Driver's Seat: The Automobile in American Literature and Popular Culture*. Westport: Greenwood, 1976.

Dickens, Charles. *American Notes for General Circulation*. 1842. New York: Penguin, 1988.

Dixon, Winifred Hawkridge. *Westward Hoboes: Ups and Downs of Frontier Motoring*. 1921. New York: Scribner's, 1928.

Dodge, Jim. *Not Fade Away*. New York: Atlantic Monthly, 1987.

Dos Passos, John. *The 42nd Parallel*. 1930. New York: New American Library, 1969.

———. *State of the Nation*. Boston: Houghton, 1944.

Dreiser, Theodore. *A Hoosier Holiday*. New York: Lane, 1916.

Duncan, Dayton. *Out West: American Journey along the Lewis and Clark Trail*. 1987. New York: Penguin, 1988.

Dunn, Katherine. *Truck*. 1971. New York: Warner, 1990.

Eco, Umberto. "Travels in Hyperreality." 1975. *Travels in Hyperreality: Essays*. Trans. William Weaver. San Diego: Harcourt, 1990. 1–58.

Eighner, Lars. *Travels with Lizbeth: Three Years on the Road and on the Streets*. New York: St. Martin's, 1993.

Ellison, Ralph. *Invisible Man*. New York: Random, 1952.

Emerson, Ralph Waldo. "The American Scholar." 1837. *Ralph Waldo Emerson: Essays and Lectures*. Ed. Joel Porte. New York: Library of America, 1983. 53–71.

———. "The Divinity School Address." 1838. *Ralph Waldo Emerson: Essays and Lectures*. Ed. Joel Porte. New York: Library of America, 1983. 73–92.

———. "Experience." 1844. *Ralph Waldo Emerson: Essays and Lectures*. Ed. Joel Porte. New York: Library of America, 1983. 471–92.

———. *Nature*. 1836. *Ralph Waldo Emerson: Essays and Lectures*. Ed. Joel Porte. New York: Library of America, 1983. 9–49.

———. "Self-Reliance." 1841. *Ralph Waldo Emerson: Essays and Lectures*. Ed. Joel Porte. New York: Library of America, 1983. 259–82.

———. "The Young American." 1844. *Ralph Waldo Emerson: Essays and Lectures*. Ed. Joel Porte. New York: Library of America, 1983. 211–32.

Eubank, Victor. "Log of an Auto Prairie Schooner: Motor Pioneers on the 'Trail to Sunset.'" *Sunset Magazine* (Feb. 1912): 188–95.

Faris, John T. *Roaming American Highways*. New York: Farrar, 1931.

Fiedler, Leslie. *Love and Death in the American Novel*. New York: Criterion, 1960.

Fink, James J. "Fordization: An Idol and its Ironies." *The Car Culture*. Cambridge MA: MIT P, 1965. 67–112.

Frazier, Ian. *Great Plains*. 1989. New York: Penguin, 1990.

Freeston, L. "Motor in Warfare." *Scribner's* 57 (Feb. 1915): 185–200.

Fuller, Chet. *I Hear Them Calling My Name: A Journey through the New South*. Boston: Houghton, 1981.

Fuller, Edmund. "An Outstanding Account of Travel Through America." Rev. of *Blue Highways*, by William Least Heat-Moon. *The Wall Street Journal* 1 Feb. 1983: 32.

Gannett, Lewis. *Sweet Land*. New York: Doubleday, 1934.

Garland, Hamlin. *Main-Travelled Roads*. Boston, 1891. Lincoln: U of Nebraska P, 1995.

Gilbert, Sandra, and Susan Gubar. *The Madwoman in the Attic: The Woman Writer and the Nineteenth Century Imagination*. New Haven: Yale UP, 1979.

Gladding, Effie Price. *Across the Continent by the Lincoln Highway*. New York: Bretano's, 1915.

Godden, Richard. *Fictions of Capital*. Cambridge: Cambridge UP, 1990.

Griffin, John Howard. *Black Like Me*. 1960, 1961. New York: New American Library, 1976.

Harris, Eddy L. *South of Haunted Dreams: A Ride through Slavery's Old Back Yard*. New York: Simon, 1993.

Harrison, Jim. *A Good Day to Die*. 1973. New York: Delta-Lawrence, 1989.

Hawthorne, Nathaniel. *The Blithedale Romance*. Boston, 1852.

Heat-Moon, William Least. *Blue Highways: A Journey into America.* 1982. New York: Fawcett Crest, 1984.

Howe, Irving. Rev. of *Invisible Man*, by Ralph Ellison. *The Nation* 174 (10 May 1952): 454.

Humphrey, Zephine [Mrs. Wallace Wier Fahnerstock]. *Green Mountains to Sierras.* New York: Dutton, 1936.

Humphreys, John R. *The Lost Towns and Roads of America.* Garden City NY: Doubleday, 1961.

Irving, Washington. *A Tour on the Prairies.* 1835. Ed. John Francis McDermott. Norman: U of Oklahoma P, 1985.

[Jackson, H. Nelson]. *From Ocean to Ocean in a Winton.* Cleveland: Winton Motor Carriage Co., [1903].

Jackson, John Brinckerhoff. *American Space.* New York: Norton, 1972.

James, Henry. *The American Scene.* 1906. Bloomington: Indiana UP, 1986.

Kaler, Anne K. *The Picara: From Hera to Fantasy Heroine.* Bowling Green OH: Bowling Green State U Popular P, 1991.

Kant, Immanuel. *Critique of Pure Reason.* Trans. N. K. Smith. New York: St. Martin's, 1965.

Kerouac, Jack. *The Dharma Bums.* 1958. New York: New American Library, 1959.
———. *On the Road.* 1957. New York: Compass Books, 1962.

Klitgaard, Kaj. *Through the American Landscape.* Chapel Hill: U of North Carolina P, 1941.

Lasch, Christopher. *The True and Only Heaven: Progress and Its Critics.* New York: Norton, 1991.

Lawrence, D. H. *Studies in Classic American Literature.* 1923. New York: Viking, 1969.

Leacock, Eleanor B., and Nancy O. Lurie, eds. *North American Indians in Historical Perspective.* New York: Random, 1971.

Leed, Eric J. *The Mind of the Traveler: From Gilgamesh to Global Tourism.* New York: Basic, 1991.

Lewis, Grace Hegger. *With Love from Gracie: Sinclair Lewis, 1912–1925.* New York: Harcourt, 1955.

Lewis, Sinclair. *Free Air.* 1919. Lincoln: U of Nebraska P, 1993.

Marx, Leo. *The Machine in the Garden*. 1964. New York: Oxford UP, 1973.

Mason, Bobbie Ann. *In Country*. 1985. New York: HarperPerennial, 1986.

Massey, Beatrice Larned. *It Could Have Been Worse: A Motor Trip from Coast to Coast*. San Francisco: Harr Wagner, 1920.

McCarthy, Eugene. *America Revisited: 150 Years after Tocqueville*. Garden City NY: Doubleday, 1978.

McMurtry, Larry. *Moving On*. New York: Simon, 1970.

———. *Cadillac Jack*. New York: Simon, 1982.

Miller, Henry. *The Air-Conditioned Nightmare*. 1945. New York: New Directions, 1970.

———. *Tropic of Cancer*. New York: Grove P, 1961.

Morris, James. *As I Saw the U.S.A*. New York: Pantheon, 1956.

Nabokov, Vladimir. *Lolita*. 1955. New York: Fawcett Crest, 1959.

Naipaul, V. S. *A Turn in the South*. 1989. New York: Vintage, 1990.

Neihardt, John G., ed. *Black Elk Speaks: Being the Life Story of a Holy Man of the Oglala Sioux*. 1932. Lincoln: U of Nebraska P, 1988.

Nicolson, Nigel, and Adam Nicolson. *Two Roads to Dodge City*. New York: Harper, 1987.

O'Gara, Geoffrey. *A Long Road Home: Journeys through America's Present in Search of America's Past*. New York: Norton, 1989.

O'Shea, Beth. *A Long Way from Boston*. New York: McGraw, 1946.

Parkman, Francis. *The Oregon Trail*. 1849. New York: New American Library, 1950.

Patton, Phil. *Open Road: A Celebration of the American Highway*. 1986. New York: Touchstone, 1987.

Percy, Walker. *The Last Gentleman*. 1966. New York: Avon, 1978.

Perrin, Noel. "By Back Roads to America." Rev. of *Blue Highways*, by William Least Heat-Moon. *The New York Times Book Review* 6 Feb. 1983: 1.

Phenix, Richard. *On My Way Home*. New York: Sloane, 1947.

Pickrel, Paul. "The Gods: Their Exits and Their Entrances." Rev. of *Around about America*, by Erskine Caldwell. *Harper's* 229 (July 1964): 103.

Pirsig, Robert M. *Zen and the Art of Motorcycle Maintenance*. 1974. New York: Bantam, 1988.

Post, Emily. *By Motor to the Golden Gate*. New York: Appleton, 1916.

Raban, Jonathan. *Hunting Mister Heartbreak*. 1991. New York: HarperPerennial, 1992.

Reeves, Richard. *American Journey: Traveling with Tocqueville in Search of "Democracy in America."* New York: Simon, 1982.

Robertson, Michael. *Beyond the Sunset*. London: Falcon P, 1950.

Rosenblum, Mort. *Back Home: A Foreign Correspondent Rediscovers America*. New York: Morrow, 1989.

Rowan, Carl. *South of Freedom*. New York: Knopf, 1954.

Saroyan, William. *Short Drive, Sweet Chariot*. N.p.: Phaedra, 1966.

Schneider, Jill. *Route 66 across New Mexico: A Wanderer's Guide*. Albuquerque: U of New Mexico P, 1991.

Sharp, Dallas Lore. *The Better Country*. Boston: Houghton, 1928.

Shelley, Percy Bysshe. "Mont Blanc." *The Norton Anthology of English Literature*. 4th ed. Vol. 1. Ed. M. H. Abrams et al. New York: Norton, 1979. 684–87. 2 vols.

Sigal, Clancy. *Going Away*. 1961. New York: Dell, 1970.

Sinclair, Upton. *The Jungle*. New York: Doubleday, 1906.

Slotkin, Richard. *Regeneration through Violence: The Mythology of the American Frontier, 1600–1860*. Middleton CT: Wesleyan UP, 1973.

Slung, Michele. "So, How Do You Like America?" *The New York Times Book Review* 17 Sept. 1989: 26.

Smith, Henry Nash. *Virgin Land: The American West as Symbol and Myth*. New York: Vintage, 1950.

Steinbeck, William. *The Grapes of Wrath*. New York: Collier, 1939.

———. *Travels with Charley: In Seach of America*. 1962. New York: Penguin, 1988.

Thompson, Jim. *Rough Neck*. 1954. New York: Mysterious P, 1989.

Thoreau, Henry David. *Walden*. 1854. *"Walden" and Other Writings of Henry David Thoreau*. Ed. Brooks Atkinson. New York: Modern Library, 1937. 3–297.

———. "Walking." 1862. *"Walden" and Other Writings of Henry David Thoreau*. Ed. Brooks Atkinson. New York: Modern Library, 1937. 597–632.

Tocqueville, Alexis Charles Henri Maurice Clerel de. *Democracy in America*. Trans. J. Spencer. New York, 1877.

Toffler, Alvin. *Future Shock*. New York: Random, 1970.

Trachtenberg, Alan. *The Incorporation of America: Culture and Society in the Guilded Age*. New York: Hill, 1983.

Travelguide: Vacation and Recreation without Humiliation. Ed. L. Nash. 1946-?.

Traven, B. *The Cotton-Pickers*. [1969?]. London: Allison, 1983.

Trollope, Frances. *Domestic Manners of the Americans*. 1832. London: Century, 1984.

Turner, Frederick Jackson. *Frontier and Section: Selected Essays of Frederick Jackson Turner*. Englewood Cliffs: Prentice, 1961.

Twain, Mark [Samuel Clemens]. *The Innocents Abroad*. Hartford, 1869.

Virilio, Paul. *Esthetique de la disparition*. Paris: Balland, 1980.

———. "A Topographical Amnesia." *The Vision Machine*. Bloomington: Indiana UP, 1994. 1–18.

Webb, Walter Prescott. *The Great Plains*. 1931. New York: Grosset, n.d.

Whitman, Walt. *Leaves of Grass. The Writings of Walt Whitman*. Vols. 1–3. New York: Putnam's, 1902. 10 vols.

———. Preface. *Leaves of Grass*. 1855. *The Heath Anthology of American Literature*. 2d ed. Vol. 1. Ed. Paul Lauter et al. Lexington MA: Heath, 1994. 2744–57. 2 vols.

Wilby, Thomas and Agnes. *On the Trail to Sunset*. New York: Moffat, 1912.

Wild, Roland. *Double-Crossing America*. London: Hale, 1938.

Williams, John A. *This Is My Country Too*. 1965. New York: New American Library, 1966.

Williams, Raymond. *The Country and the City*. New York: Oxford UP, 1973.

Winegardner, Mark. *Elvis Presley Boulevard: From Sea to Shining Sea, Almost*. New York: Atlantic Monthly, 1987.

Winn, Mary Day. *Macadam Trail: Ten Thousand Miles by Motor Coach*. New York: Knopf, 1931.

Wise, Jennings C. *The Red Man in the New World Drama*. Ed. and rev. Vine Deloria. New York: Macmillan, 1971.

Wolfe, Tom. *The Electric Kool-Aid Acid Test*. 1968. New York: Bantam, 1969.

Woolf, Douglas. *Wall to Wall*. 1962. Elmwood Park IL: Dalkey Archive, 1984.

Wright, Stephen. *Going Native*. New York: Farrar, 1994.

Index

"Resistance to Civil Government" (Thoreau), 109, 122

road books, x–xi, 30, 31–32, 68, 84; alienation in, 107, 120; consumption/production duality in, 21, 42, 60, 99, 102; contradictions in, 16; and environmental concerns, 52, 53; epiphanies in, 15–16; escape and freedom in, 14, 15–16, 24, 113; and history, 23–24, 69; influential figures of, 17–18; literary traditions of, ix, 5–15; provisioning in, 54–55, 119; rediscovery theme in, 42–48, 68, 69; revisionism in, 48–53; road consciousness in, 70–79; self-discovery in, 14, 21, 24, 28, 30, 31–32, 113, 127–28; traditions and categories of, 29–30; and walking, 101; and the West, 20, 118

road novels; character in, 131, 145; domesticity in, 131–32, 145–46, 149; self-discovery in, 145–46, 148, 149; by women, 28–29

road trips, x–xi, 1, 34; compared to railroad trips, 3–4, 33–40, 41, 42, 70, 113; and the Western frontier, 3, 4–5

Roaming American Highways (Faris), 42, 47, 66

Robertson, Michael, 71, 72, 77, 147

Rojas, Fernando de, 8

Romanticism, 9, 22, 54, 93, 113, 145; automobile and, 55, 91, 97, 108–9, 110; consciousness in, 6, 21, 38; machine and garden juxtaposed in, 41; and road books, 6–7; subject and object in, 71, 91

Roosevelt, Teddy, 14, 33

Rosenblum, Mort, 26

Rough Neck (Thompson), 11

Rousseau, Jean Jacques, 6

Route 66 across New Mexico (Schneider), 7, 66

Rowan, Carl, 18, 116, 119, 120, 126, 129

Saroyan, William, 26, 79, 92, 124; on highway consciousness, 7, 78–79; Whitman mentioned by, 83, 91, 92

satire, 18–19, 24

Schneider, Jill, 66

"Self-Reliance" (Emerson), 80, 92, 93, 112, 122

Selkirk, Alexander, 121

Sharp, Dallas Lore, 20, 27, 51, 82, 118; on the automobile, 75, 108, 124; on automobile travel, 17, 34–35; machine and garden juxtaposed by, 40–41; and the rediscovery theme, 43; revisionism of, 49; and Thoreau, 106; on train travel, 34; on travel by foot, 101–2

Shelley, Percy Bysshe, 74, 77

Short Drive, Sweet Chariot (Saroyan), 26, 78–79, 91, 92, 124

Sigal, Clancy, 14–16, 18, 51, 54; and frontier as state of mind, 45–47; and Kerouac, 19–20; mentioned, 59, 107, 119

Sinclair, Upton, 11, 119

"Song of Myself" (Whitman), 87

A Southerner Discovers the South (Daniels), 24, 26, 47, 60–61

South of Freedom (Rowan), 18, 26, 116

South of Haunted Dreams (Harris), 118, 128–29, 130

State of the Nation (Dos Passos), 20, 24, 47, 53, 60–61

Steinbeck, John, 18, 55, 70–71, 123; influence of, 17, 18; mentioned, 8, 11, 24, 27; Whitman mentioned by, 83, 87

Studies in Classic American Literature (Lawrence), 41

Thaxter, Katherine, 36, 37, 48

Theocritus, 8

This Is My Country Too (Williams), 18, 26, 119, 122

Thompson, Jim, 11, 123

Thoreau, Henry David, 104, 109, 110, 113, 123; and Eighner's *Travels with Lizbeth*, 106–7; in Humphrey's *Green Mountains to Sierras*, 105; mentioned, 6, 14, 46, 57, 96, 111, 121; and nature, 10, 81, 122; in Pirsig's *Zen*, 107; provisioning by, 54,